Praise for *Nobody's Perfect*

"This excellent collection reflects groundbreaking scholarship by young, emerging leaders in Christian religious education. In *Nobody's Perfect*, Cynthia Cameron, Lakisha Lockhart-Rusch, and Emily Peck, refusing to conflate mistakes with sin, propose a preferential option for marginalized adolescents and offer creative ways that religious educators can mentor them—even to learn from their mistakes. It will greatly benefit the faith journey of our adolescents."

—**Thomas Groome**, professor of theology and religious education, Boston College, and author of *Will There Be Faith?* and *Faith for the Heart*

"*Nobody's Perfect* is a remedy for the toxicity of what is called the perfect syndrome, a psychological malaise that disguises the privilege of white, cisgender, middle-class, adult male bodies. This book offers wisdom that validates mistakes, distinguishing them from sin and affirming them as a part of life and a source of growth. It is empowering and encouraging—a must-read for those Christian religious educators who work with adolescents, especially racialized girls and queer youth."

—**HyeRan Kim-Cragg**, principal and Timothy Eaton Memorial Church Professor of Preaching, Emmanuel College at the University of Toronto

"Starting from understanding youth as God's good creation and seeking to help each of us understand both personally and in collective and institutional spaces how to discern between mistake and sin, the authors offer pragmatic resources for learning with and from youth how we might better navigate this contested and complex world. Fully cognizant of the dynamics of intersectionality and a world infused with oppressive dynamics, these authors bring wise and insightful scholarship to bear on walking in Christian faith with youth in this world we share."

—**Mary Hess**, professor of educational leadership, Luther Seminary

"All youth should be encouraged to try things, make mistakes, and learn from them. Yet mainstream American society and Christian communities judge some youth more harshly than others. *Nobody's Perfect* challenges this judgment and makes a strong case for viewing adolescents as good and imperfect people, made in God's image, and working to be and become all that God has created them to be, mistakes and all. A must-read for all church leaders who care about and want to support young people."

—**Karen-Marie Yust**, Rowe Professor of Christian Education, Union Presbyterian Seminary

"This book challenges those who work with youth to address the impossible expectations placed on young people today, when there seems to be no option for them to make mistakes, much less learn from them. The authors of this volume bring sensitive, youth-respecting, and wise theological voices to the need to support young people in the necessary life experiences of trying and failing, erring and learning how to seek forgiveness—in short, learning to be both faithful and resilient in the face of inevitable human imperfections."

—**Joyce Ann Mercer**, professor of practical theology and pastoral care, Yale Divinity School, and author of *GirlTalk, GodTalk: Why Faith Matters to Teenage Girls—and Their Parents*

NOBODY'S PERFECT

NOBODY'S PERFECT

Redefining Sin and Mistakes in Adolescent Christian Education

Cynthia L. Cameron,
Lakisha R. Lockhart-Rusch,
and Emily A. Peck

editors

Fortress Press
Minneapolis

NOBODY'S PERFECT
Redefining Sin and Mistakes in Adolescent Christian Education

29 28 27 26 25 24   1 2 3 4 5 6 7 8 9

All Scripture quotations, unless otherwise indicated, are from the New Revised Standard Version Bible, copyright © 1989 National Council of the Churches of Christ in the United States of America. Used by permission. All rights reserved worldwide.

Chapter 7 is derived in part from "Accompanying and Learning from Reconciling United Methodist Youth at a Time of Denominational Upheaval" by Emily A. Peck-McClain, published in *Religious Education* 116, no. 5 (2021): 467–478. © Religious Education Association. Available online at https://www.tandfonline.com/DOI: 10.1080/00344087.2021.2004014, reprinted by permission of Taylor & Francis Ltd, https://www.tandfonline.com, on behalf of the Religious Education Association.

Library of Congress Cataloging-in-Publication Data

Names: Cameron, Cynthia L., editor. | Lockhart-Rusch, Lakisha R., editor. | Peck, Emily, editor.
Title: Nobody's perfect : redefining sin and mistakes in adolescent Christian education / Cynthia L. Cameron, Lakisha R. Lockhart-Rusch, and Emily A. Peck, editors.
Description: Minneapolis : Fortress Press, 2025. | Includes bibliographical references and index.
Identifiers: LCCN 2024030915 (print) | LCCN 2024030916 (ebook) | ISBN 9798889832287 (print) | ISBN 9798889832294 (ebook)
Subjects: LCSH: Sin. | Errors. | Religious education.
Classification: LCC BL475.7 .N63 2025 (print) | LCC BL475.7 (ebook) | DDC 241/.3--dc23/eng/20240919
LC record available at https://lccn.loc.gov/2024030915
LC ebook record available at https://lccn.loc.gov/2024030916

Cover design: Ashley Muehlbauer
Cover image: Closeup of white crumpled paper for texture background from Dilok Klaisataporn/Getty Images and Abstract colourful background from Jasmin Merdan/Getty Images

Print ISBN: 979-8-8898-3228-7
eBook ISBN: 979-8-8898-3229-4

To all the young people
who hope for a better world and a better church:
we see you.

Contents

Part 3
Navigating Sin and Mistakes in Culture

About the Authors

Cynthia L. Cameron holds the Patrick and Barbara Keenan Chair in Religious Education and is assistant professor of religious education at the Regis St. Michael's Faculty of Theology at the University of St. Michael's College in the University of Toronto. She received her PhD in theology and education from Boston College in 2017. Her research focuses on questions of female adolescence in theological anthropology, practices of Catholic schooling, and self-harming behaviors in adolescent girls and young women. She is the coauthor, with Christopher J. Welch, of *Life Abundant: God and the Created Order in Catholic Social Perspective*, as well as several peer-reviewed articles and book chapters. Prior to entering higher education, she had a nearly twenty-year career as a teacher and administrator in Catholic secondary schools in the United States.

Emily S. Kahm is an associate professor of theology at the College of St. Mary in Omaha, Nebraska, a women's college particularly dedicated to students who are single mothers, first generation, and/or undocumented. Her research interests include religious sexuality education, sexual ethics, theological approaches to disability, and embodiment in general. She loves making theological study practical and approachable; introductory-level classes are her favorite. She is a yarn enthusiast, a forest lover, and a mostly ineffective gardener. She lives in Omaha with her spouse and two sons.

Sarah Leer (she/her) is a native Arkansan who has served nonprofits for over a decade, including Presbyterian Church (USA) churches in Texas and Arkansas. Sarah is a graduate of Wake Forest University, Columbia Theological Seminary, and the Clinton School of Public Service. She is a practical theologian who is living into her call to deconstruct systems and disrupt the status quo in order to seek liberation, justice, and belonging in solidarity with those living on the margins. Sarah enjoys singing Broadway songs in her car, random road trips and adventures, traveling the world with friends, hanging out with her family, SEC college football, and attending youth conferences.

Lakisha R. Lockhart-Rusch is a mother, wife, daughter, sister, former Zumba instructor, playful womanist activist, and coolest auntie around. She believes in the power of play, movement, aesthetics, and creative arts in life and in theology, using the body as a locus for theological reflection. She is a consultant, executive secretary for the Religious Education Association, and, in her professorial role as assistant professor of Christian education at Union Presbyterian Seminary in Richmond, Virginia, she is not only a teacher, but a facilitator, rope jumper, game player, advocate, and catalyst for critical consciousness and engagement in educating in faith and actually living into that faith through various spiritual and artistic practices.

Jennifer Moe is associate director and postdoctoral fellow of the Young Adult Initiative at Garrett-Evangelical Theological Seminary. She received her PhD in Christian education and congregational studies from Garrett in 2018. Jennifer's research interests include the ways in which young women and girls are taught to be "good Christian women" in a variety of Christian religious subcultures and young adults in the United States and their faith practices, including how they are connected (or not) to faith communities. Dr. Moe has also served as adjunct faculty in the biblical and theological studies field at North Park University in Chicago. She currently lives in Milton, Wisconsin.

Dana Myers hasn't always been Moravian, but she came "home" in 2017 by joining Home Moravian Church in Winston-Salem, North Carolina. Dana graduated from East Carolina University with a bachelor of science in middle grades education, from Moravian Seminary with a certificate in Moravian studies, and from Luther Seminary with a master of divinity in June of 2022. Dana is an instructor for the question-persuade-refer (QPR) suicide prevention method and a facilitator for Prepare/Enrich relationship and premarital education. She is a deacon in the Moravian Church Southern Province and loves all things Moravian, especially youth ministry, Candle Tea, and Laurel Ridge. Dana is married to Matt, a sixth grade language arts teacher. Their kid,

Raine, is a junior in high school. Dana enjoys writing, all kinds of movies, and hiking the North Carolina state parks with her family. She can't wait to see what God's Next Step is for her in life and ministry.

Emily A. Peck (she/her) is mom to three kids and loves to cook, hike, and camp. She also loves seeing live music, theater, and dance, and thinks being able to do this again post-pandemic is joy embodied. Peck is visiting professor of Christian formation and young adult ministry at Wesley Theological Seminary in Washington, DC, where she is also co-director of The Hub for Collaborative and Innovative Ministry and co-director of the Children and Youth Ministry and Advocacy certificate program. She believes deeply in the power of the Spirit to help shape community. She is a graduate of Union Theological Seminary in the City of New York and Duke Divinity School. Peck is author of *Arm in Arm with Adolescent Girls: Educating into the New Creation* and a contributing editor of *We Pray with Her: Encouragement for All Women Who Lead* and *Speaking Truth: Women Lifting Their Voices in Prayer.*

David Penn is a husband, father, musician, and assistant professor of religious studies at Rivier University in Nashua, New Hampshire. He completed a PhD in practical theology from Boston University in 2019 and works at the intersection of theology, popular culture, technology, the arts, and adolescent formation. His most recent publication, a chapter in the volume *Theology, Religion, and Dystopia*, explored ways in which theology, in dialogue with popular culture, can catalyze love for the world and each other. He lives outside Boston with his family.

Christopher J. Welch is assistant professor of religious studies at Rivier University in Nashua, New Hampshire. He was awarded a PhD in theology and education by Boston College in 2018. Prior to teaching at the university level, he taught theology at the secondary school level for ten years. His research questions have always emerged from his experience with and conversation with students. Currently he has a focus on adolescent and young-adult experiences of consumer culture and of manual production. He is the coauthor, with Cynthia L. Cameron, of *Life Abundant: God and the Created Order in Catholic Social Perspective.*

Foreword

On Failing Well

Almeda M. Wright
Associate Professor of Religious Education
Yale Divinity School

Over the last few years, I have been hanging out with people in innovation and design thinking circles. From these folks, I have learned a lot about failing well. To fail well, as I understand it, is to embrace the process of trying something, making mistakes, and learning from one's mistakes. It is also about building communities and transforming cultures so that one can be supported in failing and encouraged to try again. Most good innovation and good product design in the tech and engineering world happen through significant processes of trial and error. It takes place through processes of experimentation, messing things up, having space and support to make lots of mistakes. The process also includes learning from those mistakes in ways that lead one further toward a predetermined goal or that open one to discover new ideas, new goals to pursue, and heretofore unimagined possibilities.

I was reminded of this concept of failing well as I read *Nobody's Perfect: Redefining Sin and Mistakes in Adolescent Christian Education*. I was reminded of the reality that most adolescents do not have the type of design thinking networks or culture in which they get to tinker, to really mess up, to make mistakes, to fail even, and to learn in the process. And more specifically, all too often adolescents from marginalized communities do not get the privilege of making mistakes. The stakes for them are too high. Mistakes lead to a further narrowing of opportunities or even death. Thus, too many marginalized youths wrestle with perfection because perfection seems to be the only safe way to navigate life. The authors of this book recount the ways that many youths are placed in untenable situations. And still, the authors invite us to dream together about what it would look like for every adolescent, particularly marginalized adolescents, to be taught to fail well, to have the opportunities to make mistakes without it costing them their lives or their hopes and dreams.

I was also reminded of the parallel reality that most religious communities are not set up as places to hold mistakes or even to offer robust theological reflections on mistake-making. I have struggled over the years with helping religious leaders and communities embrace mistake-making and failure as part of their stories and things that will help them grow. For the most part, religious communities, like most of our wider society, are taught to avoid mistakes and failure at all costs. Thus, it is not surprising that churches are not comfortable with failure on even small levels, or that most religious communities are not foregrounding theological conversations on how mistake-making is part of being human, or about the ways that transformation emerges in the process of making mistakes. Indeed, there is a veritable lacuna in the religious education scholarship on mistake-making. We, scholars of religious education, have not attended to this idea with the type of nuance and care required to help adults or youth navigate the mistakes they will inevitably make, nor the mistakes made by others in efforts to be in relationship with them.

The authors, however, address this lacuna and start with a robust theological foundation that adolescents are already complete and good. They reflect on the rich and complicated theological idea of the *imago Dei*, noting that adolescents are reflective of the image of God, right now. They make a bold claim that "no one images God partially, not even adolescents." I was struck by this idea because it pushes back against the myriad conscious or subconscious attempts to treat young people as deficient or undeveloped. In that statement, the conversation can shift from the work of attempting to "fix" adolescents or the mistakes that they make to other conversations. They can shift to conversations about how we might begin to see young people as full participants in their own lives, in the kin-dom of God, but also in the work of contributing fully and freely to their communities and families right now. They invite us to see the contributions and wisdom of young people, not when or if they avoid mistakes, but while they are making mistakes and learning through them with the support of their communities.

As I read through this book, I also kept thinking about what a powerful gift these authors are offering young people and religious communities. And a little selfishly, I wondered about the ways these conversations would have healed (or even eliminated) so many of the traumas that other generations of youth and adults have experienced. As I read, I kept hearing echoes of my own attempts to navigate life as a young person and as a youth worker and felt the ways that this book was a letter, a corrective, a balm to my younger self and to future generations of young people. Thus, I end with a letter to my younger self:

Dear Teenage Almeda,

You are not perfect, and that's okay. You are probably experiencing a triple bind (described by the authors) or maybe even a quadruple bind—as you are also holding together the societal expectations for what Black teenagers can and cannot do and what it means to be a good, kind, smart, confident (but not too sassy) Black girl. And yes, you are struggling with this because you want to be perfect. Some of the motivation to be perfect will come from your family, your personality, and even the theological language and images you get from your religious community. You will hear sermons about sanctification and holiness and purity—and you will wonder if you can ever live up to these standards. You will fill pages and pages of journals with your questions and struggles and fears of failing. But one day in the not-so-distant future, you will encounter mentors and spiritual guides who will help you learn that it is okay to not be perfect.

And years later, you will learn that there's a future generation of youth workers and religious education scholars who will push communities and congregations to create space for you and so many other marginalized youth to embrace the reality of making mistakes. They will help you and future generations sit with the reality that you are not perfect and that nobody is perfect and that it is not only okay, but also expected and celebrated. So, keep your head up, young Almeda, because Cynthia, Lakisha, Emily, and so many more are coming, and they are trying to build a better world and definitely better religious communities for folks like you.

Acknowledgments

This book is an expression of the passion that we have for ministering with young people. Indeed, it brings together our shared commitments to, and enthusiasms for, the process of educating in faith in a wide variety of contexts and, most importantly, for adolescents—especially the Black and brown kids, the girls, and the queer kids, the kids who oftentimes get overlooked in our teaching, ministry, and scholarship.

So, we preface this book with an acknowledgment of those who have contributed to it in ways seen and unseen. An edited volume is always the work of many hands, and this book is certainly no different. We are grateful for the people in our lives who have made this project possible: those who educated us in the Christian faith, who formed us as scholars and practitioners, who accompany us as professional colleagues, who are our students and ministry partners, who support us at home and in our families, and who encouraged us in this project.

In particular, we want to thank Yvonne D. Hawkins at Fortress Press, who guided us through the editing process and provided incredibly useful feedback. We are so grateful that she saw the same vision for this project that we did and was such a tireless advocate for it. Thanks to the Religious Education Association and the members of the working group on Adolescent Girls and Faith Formation. You gave us an institutional space in which to generate ideas and to make connections with both junior and senior colleagues. We are grateful to the peer reviewers who provided feedback to help us make this book the best it could be. Thank you as well to Kyle Ferguson and Noah MacDonald, doctoral research assistants at the Regis St. Michael's Faculty of Theology, who read and edited significant portions of this book.

Most importantly, we want to thank all of the collaborating authors of this project. Their work with, and research about, adolescents and religious education inspires hope for the future of our field. And, of course, we could not have done this without the kids, the adolescents who participated in our research, who talked with us, who are involved in our ministries, and who love us. They are our inspiration and our hope!

Introduction

Adolescents Are Good

Cynthia L. Cameron, Lakisha R. Lockhart-Rusch, and Emily A. Peck

Oftentimes, it seems like adolescents are not seen in the fullness of their humanity. In Euro-North American culture and in our churches, we tend to ignore and marginalize our adolescents. When we do think about them, we tend to think of how they need to be restrained and restricted; how they need to be protected; how they need to be shaped. We think about adolescents as problems that need to be solved rather than as human beings in their own right, created by God for communion with God and others, created in God's own image. Instead of valuing them for the unique individuals they are, we tend to focus on what is going wrong with them—the mistakes they are making or might make—without always providing them with a community within which they feel empowered to learn and to grow into healthy adults, to make and acknowledge mistakes, to hold others accountable for their mistakes, and to begin to think theologically about both mistakes and sin.

Christian theologies of sin often stand in the way of the efforts of religious educators to affirm the goodness of adolescents and to accompany them as they grow toward a healthy adult faith. When Christian churches and institutions focus too narrowly on sin—as missing the mark, as falling short of expectations, as personal choice—we miss an opportunity to talk with adolescents about the role that mistakes play in our learning processes. We know that young people will make mistakes and we claim that we want them to learn from these mistakes. But we make that process harder for them when we conflate mistakes and sin. Not everything a person does that is wrong is, in fact, a sin. We all make lots of unintentional errors of judgment, do good things less well than we had hoped, and do things by accident. We are also all learning and growing, no matter our age, and part of that growth comes from making and learning from mistakes. Because of their lack of experience with navigating the theological tradition, adolescents may have a harder time telling the difference between sins and mistakes than do some adults, especially those who have a depth of theological knowledge on which to draw.

This creates an opportunity for Christian religious educators to explore this distinction with the young people under their care. And, importantly, it provides us with the opportunity to make a preferential option for marginalized adolescents, to focus on the voices of those adolescents who are most often excluded from and marginalized in religious education and church spaces. Teenage girls, LGBTQIA+ youth, and adolescents of color, therefore, deserve to be centered in the thinking of scholars of Christian religious education and in the ministry of religious educators. Focusing on marginalized adolescents reveals the ways that traditional Christian language of sin is rooted in patriarchal and racist presumptions and how our field has too often assumed that the white, cisgender, straight, middle-class boy is the paradigmatic adolescent, able to stand in for all adolescents. Christian educators can disrupt this assumption with a conscious attention to all the many and wonderful ways that our adolescents are embodied. They are not a one-size-fits-all category of human; they deserve a Christian religious education that recognizes and affirms their diversity.

So, how is mistake-making taught to adolescents? How do they understand their own actions in light of traditional Christian theologies of sin? What do adolescents want their Christian religious educators and youth ministers to know about sin and mistakes that they are not currently learning or putting into practice in their own lives? In light of these questions, scholars and practitioners of Christian religious education can assist adolescents in various settings in the United States, the adults who work with them, the faith communities they belong to. We can expand the conversation in Christian religious education to take account of the often-challenging culture of the United States so that we can better accompany adolescents as they grow toward a healthy adult faith. We can educate toward the kin-dom of God[1] and journey with adolescents in more loving ways.

Adolescence in the Twenty-First Century

Today's young people face challenges that were not faced—or at least not faced in the same way—by generations that came before. Social science researchers who focus on adolescent development within communities often paint a grim picture for us—one that ought to be particularly troubling for those of us who work with adolescents in churches and church-related institutions. Political scientist Robert Putnam notes that, while our culture's individualism has a negative effect on adults and makes building supportive communities difficult, this cultural shift to individualism, consumerism, and busyness ends up leaving young people without the communities of support that they need.[2] If it is true that it takes a village to raise a child, we find ourselves in a time when those villages no longer exist and families are largely on their own to figure out how to raise children and adolescents to a healthy adulthood. Young people are no longer known to the people in their communities beyond the formal relationships of parent, teacher, pastor, or coach; at the same time, generally, adults in the community no longer feel a responsibility to watch over teens that they are not related to or paid to be with.[3]

---

1 This phrase, an adaptation of the theological symbol of the "kingdom/reign of God," was coined by Cuban American mujerista theologian Ada Maria Isasi-Diaz as a way of problematizing the imperialism and dominance inherent in the traditional formulation. As an alternative, "kin-dom" highlights God's activity in and orientation toward familial care, inclusion, solidarity, and unity. See Ada Maria Isasi-Diaz, "Kin-dom of God: A Mujerista Proposal," in *In Our Own Voices: Latino/a Renditions of Theology*, ed. Benjamin Valentin (Maryknoll, NY: Orbis Books, 2010); Ada Maria Isasi-Diaz, *Mujerista Theology: A Theology for the Twentieth Century* (Maryknoll, NY: Orbis Books, 1996).

2 Robert D. Putnam, *Our Kids: The American Dream in Crisis* (New York: Simon & Schuster, 2015). See also Robert D. Putnam, *Bowling Alone: The Collapse and Revival of American Community* (New York: Simon & Schuster, 2000).

3 Putnam, *Our Kids*, 4. It is important to note that Putnam is not suggesting that we should return to the supposed "golden age" of the mid-twentieth century when these structures last existed. In fact, there were significant ways in which this kind of community orientation failed young people—silencing those seen as "other" because of race, gender and gender identity, and sexual orientation—and reinforced a sense of forced communal cohesiveness.

In addition, as psychologist Richard Lerner describes, our culture's approach to teenagers in the late twentieth and early twenty-first centuries is one where we rather unconsciously treat adolescents as problems to be solved. Adult interaction with adolescents (in families, schools, churches, and communities) is one that seeks to prevent the bad as opposed to nurturing the good in adolescents.[4] The work of child psychologist David Elkind and religious educator Chap Clark suggests that a key factor in this deficit approach to adolescence is a shift in the ways we see the world from one where children and adolescents were understood as immature members of the community who needed to be nurtured into their eventual adult roles to one that focuses almost exclusively on adults.[5] In this shift, not only are children and adolescents isolated from caring adults around them (sent to schools, sent to youth groups, signed up for extra activities, and so on), they are also forced to engage the adult world without sufficient modeling of how to do this by the adults in their families. In fact, as therapist Martha Straus notes, adolescents spend remarkably little time with adult family members.[6] This sense of isolation described by social scientists is often also found in our churches. Religious educator David White suggests that adolescents are routinely separated from the adults of the church community; they do not get to see what being an adult in the church means because, outside of the worship services, they do not get to see adults engaged in the work of the church. Adolescents

---

4 Richard M. Lerner, *The Good Teen: Rescuing Adolescence from the Myths of the Storm and Stress Years* (New York: Three Rivers Press, 2007). Lerner summarizes this approach: "All too often, [adults] have acted as if the only important aspect of their children's behaviors were those that caused problems. We think of adolescence as a time of storm and stress. Scientists, too, have regarded young people as lacking, as deficient, as unable to behave correctly and in a healthy manner. We characterize them as dangerous to others and as endangered themselves (because of their self-destructive behaviors)" (3).

5 See David Elkind, *All Grown Up and No Place to Go: Teenagers in Crisis*, rev. ed. (Cambridge, MA: Perseus Books, 1998); Chap Clark, *Hurt 2.0: Inside the World of Today's Teenagers* (Grand Rapids, MI: Baker Academic, 2011); Theresa O'Keefe, "Growing Up Alone: The New Normal of Isolation in Adolescence," *The Journal of Youth Ministry* 13, no. 1 (Fall 2014): 63–84.

6 Martha B. Straus, *Adolescent Girls in Crisis: Intervention and Hope* (New York: W. W. Norton, 2007), 7–8.

are told that they are the future of the church and not that they are the church.[7]

At the same time, adolescents live with many of the same challenges as adults do. The Christian message of communal care, hospitality, solidarity, and responsibility for one another can easily and often get lost in the Euro-North American emphases on individualism and consumerism. Both teenagers and adults are formed by this culture in which we all live and, because of their isolation from the web of relationships that could support them, teenagers do not always know how to navigate these cultural pressures.

Consumerism, in particular, forms and shapes the ways that adolescents understand their identities and their role in wider society. Around the world, children and adolescents are exploited and manipulated by the global capitalist system.[8] And, while adolescents in the United States are not significant earners in our society (although many of them do have jobs either to help provide for their families or for extra spending money), advertisers long ago identified teens as a key demographic and companies vie for teen dollars. Teens are drawn into this culture of consumerism and materialism without the adult guidance that would help them reflect on the historical and systemic issues that get played out in their spending habits. Most teens are unaware, for example, of the connections between their patterns of buying and the American legacy of slavery, racial restrictions on economic participation during segregation, the ways that women were and continue to be excluded from workforce participation and access to credit, the increasing costs of quality childcare and unequal access to healthcare, and more. Racism, sexism, classism, and many other systemic evils are rooted in and supported by our economic and consumer decisions.[9] And, because

---

7 David F. White, *Practicing Discernment with Youth: A Transformative Youth Ministry Approach* (Cleveland, OH: Pilgrim Press, 2005), 24–25.

8 For a helpful analysis of child labor and consumption, see Mary M. Doyle Roche, *Children, Consumerism, and the Common Good* (Lanham, MD: Lexington Books, 2009).

9 See Andrea Flynn, *The Hidden Rules of Race: Barriers to an Inclusive Economy* (New York: Cambridge University Press, 2017); Susan Thistle, *From Marriage to the Market: The Transformation of Women's Lives and Work* (Berkeley: University of California Press, 2006).

teens are in large part on their own when dealing with consumer culture, they do not see the ways that their choices have consequences that impact people that may seem quite far removed from their day-to-day lives. Similarly, they also may consider themselves to be internet savvy but do not necessarily have a critical eye to how they are being advertised to by influencers in their social media circles.

The challenges faced by contemporary adolescents are not only about our economic system, however. Teenagers, like all other participants in US culture, are formed in and through the racism, xenophobia, sexism, and heterosexism that make up this culture. In the United States, the bodies that people inhabit make a difference for privilege and risk; the disparities that are built into our systems mean that social location makes a significant difference in the outcomes of mistake-making. All too often, white people are allowed to make mistakes, and Black, brown, and other people of color often suffer much graver consequences—up to and including extra-judicial execution—because of their own mistakes and the mistakes of others. We can call to mind stories of unarmed Black teenagers being shot by white adults for the so-called mistake of playing with a toy gun, as in the case of Tamir Rice, or walking with a hoodie on, as in the case of Trayvon Martin. White college student Brock Turner's sexual assault of an unconscious woman received a slap-on-the-wrist sentence because the judge did not want his youthful indiscretions to derail a promising future. Transgender adolescents have to fight to participate in their chosen sports and to use the bathrooms and locker rooms where they feel most safe; their very identities are named by some in society as mistaken and wrong, and, by some, even as sinful. Some Americans get to make mistakes and others do not; some Americans are labeled as mistakes and others are not.

As Christians and as a Christian community, however, we are called to a different vision of how we can treat each other and live together. This is a vision that counters the isolation, individualism, consumerism, and systemic injustices that are characteristic of the contemporary US context. It is a call to participate in the creation of the kin-dom of God, a kin-dom that is attested to in the teachings, ministry, and community of Jesus. As religious educator Thomas Groome reminds us, this is the vision toward which we educate and by which we are inspired.[10] If the gospel message is one of kinship, hospitality, community, and justice, then the church is called to educate its young people toward this vision of what it means to be a human person in relationship with God, others, self, and all of creation. And we are called to resist the cultural pressures that privilege some and put those deemed "other" at greater risk.

Therefore, as we consider the responsibilities of Christian religious education to our adolescents, we want to participate in building up church communities that are oriented toward helping adolescents not just survive, but flourish in our contemporary context. As scholars and practitioners of religious education, we are called to provide teens with the tools for understanding, reflecting on, and responding to what the contemporary US culture is telling them about mistakes and mistake-making. The church, its ministers, and its formation programs have a responsibility to help teens navigate their culture in ways that help them grow toward a healthy adulthood. We want teenagers to know that they, like everyone else, will make mistakes in their lives; they will also sin. Individuals, institutions, churches, and even society as a whole will make mistakes and will sin in ways that will affect teenagers. Thus, one of the tasks of adolescent faith development is coming to terms with their own mistakes, mistakes made by those they love and respect, mistakes that are codified into our country's norms and laws, and mistakes made by their churches.

A Theology of Adolescence

In order to think theologically about mistake-making for twenty-first-century adolescence, we must name a core theological commitment shared by all of the authors who contributed to this book: *adolescents*

---

10 Thomas H. Groome, *Sharing Faith: A Comprehensive Approach to Religious Education* (San Francisco: HarperSanFrancisco, 1991). Groome writes that, in Christian religious education, it is the Christian Story/Vision that "affirms questions and calls [people] beyond their own and their society's present praxis" (123). Part of how this happens in his method of Christian religious education is placing people's stories/visions into conversation with the Christian Story/Vision, a story that calls the church to those qualities of community and justice.

already embody the fullness of humanity and are fundamentally good. To ground this commitment, Christian religious educators need a capacious theological understanding of our young people. If the church is called to help adolescents make sense of one of the primary characteristics of what it means to be human—the universal tendency to make mistakes, commit sins, and participate in sinful systems—then we need to spend some time reflecting on our overarching theological vision of adolescents as fully human beings, created by God. For this, the theological symbol of the *imago Dei*, that human beings are created by God in the image and likeness of God (Genesis 1:27), can form the foundation of a robust theological anthropological understanding of our adolescents.

In many of our churches' traditional theological anthropologies, the model for the human person is the white, straight, cisgender, middle-class, middle-aged male. Those who do not fit this model have traditionally been excluded from or marginalized in our theological reflection. While a great deal of important contextual work has been done to reorient our theological vision so that race, gender, and class are explicitly taken up,[11] age—and the experiences of marginalization associated with age—has not generally been explored by theologians.[12] Thus, our dominant view of what counts as a "complete" or "worthy" human person is still the middle-aged adult.

However, as one of the foundational theological beliefs about the human person, the doctrine of the *imago Dei* can move us away from a deficit model of thinking about adolescents, transforming our thinking of them as problems to be solved into thinking of them as fully human beings, created and loved by God and full members of the church and the world. The *imago Dei* doctrine, then, becomes the lens through which we see adolescents, not simply as sinners who need to be corrected, as clay that needs to be shaped, or as seedlings that need to be

11 For a summary of this work, see Michelle A. Gonzalez, *Created in God's Image: An Introduction to Feminist Theological Anthropology* (Maryknoll, NY: Orbis Books, 2007), particularly chapters 4 and 5. And, as Grace Kim and Susan Shaw remind us, the intersections of multiple identities are an important theological consideration. See Grace Ji-Sun Kim and Susan M. Shaw, *Intersectional Theology: An Introductory Guide* (Minneapolis: Fortress Press, 2018).

12 Cynthia L. Cameron, "You Are the Now of God: *Christus Vivit* and the Need for a Theological Anthropology of Youth," *Horizons* 50, no. 1 (June 2023): 110–135.

nurtured, but as fully human persons in their own right who bring into theological view some of the many aspects of our shared humanity. The doctrine allows us to affirm that being created by God in the image of God is not something that we attain at adulthood. One does not grow into the *imago Dei*. The *imago Dei* is not something that develops in us. Nor is it something that could decline as we age. No one images God partially, not even adolescents.

A theological anthropology focused on the *imago Dei* that takes adolescence seriously provides us with three very useful perspectives that will ground the theological reflections of this book. The first is that this forces us into a positive theological anthropology. Unlike our theological forbearers, many of whom saw childhood as an illness,[13] and our culture, which views adolescents as problems to be solved or a market to exploit, a positive theological anthropology reminds us that adolescents are good. Because they, like all human beings, are created in the image of God, they are loved by God and created by God for flourishing.[14] A positive theological anthropology of adolescence acknowledges that no person is a mistake; creation in God's image means that the variety amongst humans—variety revealed in gender and gender identity, race, and sexual orientation, among other forms—is a part of God's intention for humanity. Moreover, it affirms for us that adolescents cannot be assumed to be sinful or deficient; thus, adolescents are not their mistakes. As with all people, the mistakes made by young people are a part of their experiences as human beings created by God; any theological approach that limits our acceptance of or love for adolescents because of the mistakes they make is itself sinful: it violates our commitment to the innate goodness of the human person and to the full flourishing of all people.

---

13 See Jerome W. Berryman, *Children and the Theologians: Clearing the Way for Grace* (New York: Morehouse Publishing, 2009). Berryman notes that Augustine, John Calvin, and Jonathan Edwards, in particular, saw children as fundamentally evil. Other theologians, including Thomas Aquinas and Martin Luther, saw potential for a grace-filled life in children, but did not see childhood itself as good.

14 Feminist theologian Elizabeth Johnson names flourishing as a key criterion of contemporary theology. See Elizabeth A. Johnson, *She Who Is: The Mystery of God in Feminist Theological Discourse*, 10th anniv. ed. (New York: Herder & Herder, 2002), 30–31.

A second useful perspective for an understanding of adolescence in theological anthropology is the affirmation that the *imago Dei* is a corporate, rather than only an individual, identity. Being created in the image of God is a statement about the whole person and the whole community, and about the role of humanity within the whole cosmos, and not merely about the particular characteristics that we may display at any given moment. So, when we speak of the *imago Dei*, it is important to remember that we are talking about both individual persons who are created in the image of God and about humanity in general.[15] This means that, while each person reflects something of the image of God in their life, the totality of what it means to be created in the image of God can only come into view when we look to all of humanity. For our explorations of the mistake-making of adolescents and the mistakes of the cultures and institutions of which they are a part, this perspective forces us to recognize both the individuality and the corporate identity of young people. So, churches *need* adolescents and their unique experiences—including their experiences of mistake-making and being victims of the mistakes of others—in order for the image of God as a corporate identity of the whole of humanity to come into theological view. This also means that we cannot paint all adolescents as "bad" because of the poor choices of some; each young person is a unique expression of the *imago Dei* with their own human dignity which needs to be respected. Similarly, not every characteristic associated with humanity as created in the image of God must be found in each and every adolescent person. So, we cannot expect every adolescent to express their humanity—including their mistake-making—in the same way.

Finally, creation in the image of God undergirds a renewed appreciation in contemporary theology for the goodness of human embodiment. The theological tradition has typically ignored the role that different bodies make in people's experiences of injustice and oppression and in their hopes and expectations for the kin-dom of God. Contextual theologians, particularly womanist, queer, mujerista, and feminist theologians, rightly challenge the traditional erasure of

---

15 Evangelical theologian John Kilner is very helpful in this distinction. See John F. Kilner, *Dignity and Destiny: Humanity in the Image of God* (Grand Rapids, MI: Eerdmans Publishing, 2015).

differing embodiment from theological view. They are challenging a perspective, perpetuated in both theology and in the wider culture, that bodies are troublesome at best. Moreover, Black and brown bodies and the bodies of women and LGBTQIA+ adolescents are policed, controlled, and assaulted as a way of corralling those deemed different or other than a white, cisgender, middle-aged, middle-class male body. As theologian Mary Doak reminds us, "to discuss embodiment without race and gender . . . contradicts the claim that diversity is central to the divine intention. Furthermore, when theological anthropology proceeds as though androcentric and Eurocentric experiences are sufficient to understand human reality, those who are not among the white, male, Euro-American elite are devalued."[16] Womanist theologian M. Shawn Copeland goes further, suggesting that honoring bodies, particularly Black bodies, is an honoring of our humanity; conversely, to fail to honor bodies is to deny our "specificity as God's human creatures, made in God's own image and likeness."[17] Bringing adolescent embodiment into view means not only acknowledging the embodied changes that adolescent bodies are experiencing as they develop into physical and sexual maturity; it also means recognizing the ways that experiences of embodiment influence how teens understand their own mistakes and the messages about mistake-making that they receive from the culture and the church. Our adolescents need messages from the church in general and from the adults charged with their faith formation in particular that their bodies are created by God and intended by God for good. They need to hear from us that they are good in all their embodied glory.

Nobody's Perfect

This book, then, is an exploration of what mistake-making and sin mean for adolescents and the adults who work with them in faith-based communities: religious schooling, such as Catholic schools; formal educative programming at parishes, such as Sunday school or youth group;

---

16 Mary Doak, "Sex, Race, and Culture: Constructing Theological Anthropology for the Twenty-First Century," *Theological Studies* 80, no. 3 (2019): 528.

17 M. Shawn Copeland, *Enfleshing Freedom: Body, Race, and Being* (Minneapolis: Fortress Press, 2010), 18.

the more informal formation that happens in the day-to-day ministries of churches, and the sometimes unintentional formation that happens outside of the institutional church. We come at these questions from different angles and we consider different populations of adolescents, but we share a conviction that the Christian community can think together about our commitments to form adolescents, and indeed all people, in faith. And that, if we do so, the Christian community can grow toward being the more just place that all of our adolescents, and particularly girls, LGBTQIA+ teens, and racialized youth, need.[18]

This book is divided into three parts. While each part—and, indeed, each chapter—is able to stand on its own, it is in the connections among all three parts that one is able to see the depth and nuance involved in any consideration of adolescents, mistake-making, and Christian religious education.

First, part 1—"Distinguishing Sin from Mistakes"—explores how adolescents and the adults who work with them define mistake-making, definitions that are then put into conversation with understandings of sin. The four chapters in this part seek to draw a sharper distinction between mistake-making and sinning in order to better name the lived experiences of adolescents. Drawing on both qualitative and quantitative research, the chapters collectively argue for more nuanced and robust definitions of sin and mistake as religious educators help young people navigate some of the difficult choices of their growing up.

In chapter 1, "The Rhetoric of Relationships, Sin, and Mistake-Making," Cynthia Cameron describes the experiences of adolescent girls in Catholic secondary schools while exploring the contributions of feminist theologians to the construction of a more adequate theology of sin that speaks into these girls' experiences. Emily S. Kahm continues this reflection on the experiences of adolescent girls in chapter 2, "Mistake and Sin in Adolescent Sexuality," in which she argues that the inadequate sexuality education received by girls—in fact, a mistake made by parents and educators—is rooted in the tendency to treat all adolescent sexual behavior as a mistake or sin. In chapter 3, "Christian Girlhood Books and Evangelical Culture," Jennifer Moe argues that

---

18 The authors and editors of this book take a broad understanding of terms relating to individual identity. We follow the lead of research subjects in their self-identified pronouns and terms for expressing their sexualities and gender identifications.

books aimed at adolescent girls and popularized in Evangelical communities reinscribe a patriarchal worldview by advising girls that Christian womanhood calls them to be obedient, quiet, unassuming, and good. Drawing part one to a close, David Penn's chapter 4, "Companioning Youth through Their Mistakes," interrogates the language used by faith communities to talk with adolescents about mistake-making, suggesting that what counts as a mistake is socially constructed.

The second part of the book, "Navigating Institutional Mistake-Making," suggests that an important part of the challenge of talking about mistake-making with adolescents is that their institutional contexts—through policy, pastoral practice, and ministry orientations—often give lie to our explicit messages. By bringing a particular focus to practices of LGBTQIA+ exclusion in churches, these three chapters explore the impacts that institutional sinfulness and mistake-making impacts the faith and well-being of adolescent members of those institutions.

In chapter 5, "Queerness in Light of God's Goodness in Creation," Dana Myers argues that, too often, LGBTQIA+ youth hear messages from the church that *they* are mistakes because of their sexuality or gender identity and she calls pastors and religious educators to proclaim a theological narrative of affirmation. Also taking seriously the experiences of queer teens, Sarah Leer's chapter 6, "Creating Communities of Belonging with LGBTQIA+ Youth," argues that churches that want to be welcoming of LGBTQIA+ people must enact belonging in their spaces through subversive, decolonial practices. In chapter 7—"Youth Leadership for the Church"—Emily Peck explores the tension that exists when young people object to the teachings of a denomination of which they are a part and how they can help lead the church to more faithful inclusion. While all three of these chapters are grounded in particular denominational experiences, they provide insight into the needs of LGBTQIA+ adolescents and what these adolescents can teach the broader Christian community about resisting institutional sin and mistakes.

Finally, part 3 of the book—"Navigating Sin and Mistakes in Culture"—explores the ways that young people understand and process what mistake-making looks like in the particular contexts in which they live and learn. Spaces designed for learning, whether formal church spaces or informal religious education experiences, offer an opportunity to accompany adolescents in a justice-oriented praxis of flourishing despite, or even because of, mistakes.

Lakisha R. Lockhart-Rusch interrogates the concept of safe space and explores the differences in safety between white adolescents and adolescents of color in chapter 8, "The Color of Safety for Black and Brown Youth," proposing that churches and spaces of religious education be creative spaces that encompass dialogue, conflict, honesty, and justice for all adolescents. In chapter 9, "When Consumer Culture Is the Mistake," Christopher Welch explores the ways that youth learn from both the adults in their lives and from the cultural milieu in which both are embedded, inviting religious educators to problematize consumer culture and to invite youth into a vision for a more abundant life, and to begin to transform the culture.

With this more robust understanding of the mistakes made by adolescents and those they observe and sometimes participate in in their communities, we hope that religious educators and other pastoral ministers can attend more fully to the flourishing of young people in our faith communities. And we hope that we can help teens and those who accompany them to put mistake-making into theological and pastoral context, to affirm that all teens are loved by God, and, ultimately to rejoice in how good adolescents are.

Part One

Distinguishing Sin from Mistakes

CHAPTER ONE

The Rhetoric of Relationships, Sin, and Mistake-Making

Cynthia L. Cameron

The ways that we teach girls about sin and mistakes matters. Catholic schools, in particular, because they are one of the key faith-based institutions in the lives of their students, have a responsibility to help adolescent girls tease out the differences between sinning and making mistakes. Girls are socialized by their contemporary culture to prioritize the formation and maintenance of relationships, and this cultural dynamic can often form girls into ways of thinking about their own behavior that leads them to misunderstand sin and whether their own actions are sinful. The adults who work with girls in Catholic schools, particularly those tasked with Catholic faith formation, have an opportunity to clarify for girls the role of relationships in their moral decision-making and the difference between sin and mistake.

Indeed, psychologist Stephen Hinshaw describes the social context of girls as an experience of a "triple bind," in which girls find themselves held to three powerful and contradictory sets of expectations: to succeed at all the typically "girl things" (being caring and nurturing), all the typically "boy things" (being competitive and assertive), and to conform to a narrow vision of feminine beauty.[1] In this context, the

---

1 Stephen Hinshaw with Rachel Kranz, *The Triple Bind: Saving Our Teenage Girls from Today's Pressures and Conflicting Expectations* (New York: Ballantine Books, 2009), xii–xiii.

Roman Catholic Church's[2] contemporary language of sin as a violation of relationship needs careful nuancing in order to be more helpful for girls. Without this nuancing, the Church's theological approach runs the risk of reinforcing a sexist approach to sin and to female adolescence. In conversation with adult teachers, ministers, and student life professionals who work with girls in Catholic schools, I suggest that those who work with adolescent girls in schools, churches, and other Christian faith-based institutions can be attentive to the experiences of girls as they help them navigate the sometimes fuzzy boundary between sin and mistake.[3]

Girlhood and Twenty-First-Century Patriarchy

The United States in the twenty-first century would seem to be the ideal place and time to be an adolescent girl. Adolescent girls are told that they have an equality of access, a sense of freedom to be whatever they want to be, and the opportunities to participate in the world and to make a difference. Despite these messages of limitless possibilities, girls still find themselves navigating a patriarchal culture that shapes the ways that they understand their identity, their relationships, and their futures.[4] Nearly thirty years ago, psychologist Mary Pipher named what researchers had been seeing for some time and continue to see: that many adolescent girls are in serious trouble, that they are less confident, less outgoing, and more unhappy.[5] Pipher aligns the unhappiness of girls with a realization of their own lack of power in a patriarchal

---

2 Here and throughout the chapter, I use "Church" and "Catholic Church" synonymously.

3 This study was approved by the Institutional Review Board of Rivier University, Nashua, NH. While the study originally intended to focus on the voices of the girls, the complexities of the COVID-19 pandemic required a shift to speaking with the adult members of Catholic school communities. Using Zoom, I interviewed twelve Catholic school employees from four different Catholic high schools (two coeducational and two single-sex) in the northeastern part of the United States: seven theology teachers, two campus ministers, one counselor, and three other student-life professionals (dean of students, activities director, service program coordinator). Throughout, I use pseudonyms for these interviewees.

4 Hinshaw, *The Triple Bind*, 15–18.

5 Mary Pipher, *Reviving Ophelia: Saving the Selves of Adolescent Girls* (New York: Grosset/Putnam, 1994), 19.

culture; they come to realize "that men have the power and that [girls'] only power comes from consenting to become submissive adored objects. . . . Adolescent girls experience a conflict between their autonomous selves and their need to be feminine, between their status as human beings and their vocation as females."[6] Pipher names for us that the problems of adolescent girls are not merely the isolated problems of individual girls; rather they speak to the toxicity of the culture in which girls are growing to adulthood.[7]

The relentless pressure of this sexist and patriarchal culture places girls in what Hinshaw has named as a triple bind. Girls find themselves held to three sets of expectations that are contradictory and impossible to meet. First, girls are expected to be good at all the traditional "girl stuff" like friendships and relationship building and being nice, obedient, cooperative, helpful, and nurturing. They are expected to attract boys and be good girlfriends while at the same time knowing how to manage their own sexual feelings and those of their boyfriends.[8]

> The essence of these girl skills is maintaining relationships: doing what others expect of you while putting [others'] needs first. It's the quality that leads a girl to spend all evening talking a friend through a crisis rather than using those hours to write her own A-level paper. It's also

---

6 Pipher, *Reviving Ophelia*, 21–22; Patricia H. Davis, *Counseling Adolescent Girls* (Minneapolis: Fortress Press, 1996), 18.

7 Hinshaw draws the analogy: "Imagine what might happen if we forced our teenage daughters to remain for several hours each day in a room that was full of cigarette smoke. Distasteful (and unethical) though this would be, the vast majority would probably emerge relatively intact. Yes, some would develop lung cancer (probably those with genetic vulnerabilities), and a few more would come down with emphysema, asthma, bronchitis, and other respiratory ailments as a direct or indirect result of the smoke. . . . Most, however, would not require medical care or hospital treatment. But does that mean they would be truly okay?" (Hinshaw, *The Triple Bind*, xvi.)

8 Rooted in the patriarchal culture, this aspect of the triple bind assumes heterosexuality among girls, that they are most interested in forming romantic relationships with boys. In fact, as Hinshaw argues, this presumed heterosexuality not only norms the heterosexual experience and prioritizes the needs of heterosexual boys, it also obscures the experiences of girls with other sexual orientations, limiting their ability to explore other sexual expressions. I would add that this also marginalizes those adolescents whose gender identity or gender expression does not fit into the neat binary of the triple bind; the expectations of "feminine" behavior and appearance assume both heterosexuality and cisgender. See Hinshaw, *The Triple Bind*, 8–9.

the quality that might lead her to suppress her own abilities or desires in order to boost a boyfriend's ego or reassure an anxious parent.[9]

Second, girls are expected to be good at all the things that have traditionally been the domain of boys. They are expected to play sports, compete for school government offices, fight to get into a top college, seek and succeed at a competitive career. Girls are told that they should be "a winner at anything you undertake, regardless of your own or others' feelings."[10] And girls are expected to approach dating in the ways that many boys do, engaging in multiple brief and casual sexual encounters that are devoid of meaning and relationship.[11] Third, girls are expected to do all of this while conforming to an unrealistic standard for what is expected of women's appearances. It is no longer enough for women to be kind and nurturing while at the same time being competitive and successful; they must also "fit the ever-narrower standards for looking pretty, hot, and model-thin."[12]

The triple bind is particularly insidious because it disguises the narrowing of options for girls in this veneer of a proliferation of choices. Girls are told they can have any career they want, but only as long as they do it perfectly and in the way the culture demands by mastering all the relationship-building tasks assigned to women while looking like they've stepped out of a magazine. A girl cannot be mostly nurturing or a little bit competitive or moderately good looking; today's adolescent girls are under pressure to be the perfect friend, daughter, and girlfriend, the perfect athlete, leader, and student, and the perfectly thin and sexy woman. Not only do girls have to be perfect at all three aspects of the triple bind, they also have to make it all seem effortless. Girls are being asked to "present their appearance, their abilities, and their unique identities not as the product of enormous labor but as the

---

9 Hinshaw, *The Triple Bind*, 7.

10 Hinshaw, *The Triple Bind*, 8.

11 Hinshaw, *The Triple Bind*, xii. For a discussion of hook-up culture, especially as it is played out at the college level, see Donna Freitas, *The End of Sex: How Hookup Culture Is Leaving a Generation Unhappy, Sexually Unfulfilled, and Confused* (New York: Basic Books, 2013). For an account of how this culture is experienced by high school–aged girls and how it is impacted by internet use, see Nancy Jo Sales, *American Girls: Social Media and the Secret Lives of Teenagers* (New York: Alfred Knopf, 2016).

12 Hinshaw, *The Triple Bind*, xiii.

'natural' expression of their inner beauty."[13] In the triple bind, the culture is not only narrowing the definition of what it means to be a successful woman, it is also eliminating the choices for those women who might want to resist this vision of womanhood.[14] It is saying to girls that there is only one way to be a woman and that no other constructions of womanhood or femininity are acceptable. And girls often feel like they are disappointing someone if they fail to fully live up to these expectations. They are often frustrated, anxious, overwhelmed, sad, and tired.[15]

Many of the teachers I interviewed echo Hinshaw's analysis of the triple bind. Mia, a white theology teacher in her fifties, commented that she is very concerned about the increasing pressures put on her students.

> When I was in high school, I was not one of the cool girls. And that was okay in my girls' school. But I look at my female students today and I know I couldn't live their lives. They have so many activities and they study into the wee hours every night—all to get into a good college. They worry about how to be a good friend and a good girlfriend when they have so little free time; they are sad that they don't spend regular downtime with their families; they worry that their hair is wrong or that their breasts are too small or their waist is too large. They spend too much time watching YouTube makeup tutorials and they waste their money on heaps of makeup, trying to attract that illusive "perfect" boy. And this is just the anxiety I know about.

Andrew, a white man who is a Catholic priest and campus minister, noted that "the girls are always so exhausted all of the time; they are

---

13 Hinshaw, *The Triple Bind*, 64.

14 Hinshaw, *The Triple Bind*, 8–9. Hinshaw argues that "girls used to be able to escape the narrow demands of femininity through such alternative roles as beatnik, tomboy, intellectual, hippie, punk, or goth. They'd embrace the ideals of feminism to proclaim that women didn't always have to be pretty, nice, and thin. ... Or girls might follow a counterculture that challenged the notion of ascending the corporate ladder or fulfilling men's notions of the ideal woman. They'd imitate pop stars who presented alternate looks and styles of femininity: Janis Joplin, Patti Smith, Tina Turner, Cyndi Lauper. They'd take up basketball or hockey; they'd turn into bookworms or dream of being president. All of these alternatives to traditional female roles gave independent girls a little breathing room" (8–9).

15 Martha B. Straus, *Adolescent Girls in Crisis: Intervention and Hope* (New York: W.W. Norton, 2007), 10–16.

trying to do it all and it is exhausting." Suzanne, a Latina counselor, noted that she is seeing more and more girls who say that they are overwhelmed by the unwritten expectations:

> They entered into high school and mid-adolescence assuming they had the skills it took to be a teenage girl. But so many of them are finding the expectations to be crazy and they feel like they are letting people down all the time. The B on the test, not making the team, getting into a fight with a friend. They feel like everything makes them a disappointment to the people who love them."

The triple bind is both a result of a patriarchal culture and reinforces that culture. As women seemed to be gaining ground in the fight for equality with men, the triple bind has functioned to limit women's choices. Women who must master all three aspects of the triple bind are no longer a threat to men or male power. When girls are taught that the only way to be a success is to be perfect at everything, then they, and those around them, are justified in treating them as less than successful when they do not meet these standards of perfection. The subtle messages of a patriarchal culture are still there: women must take care of others, particularly men and children; women must look the way men want them to look and act the way men want them to act; women must fashion themselves to meet the desires of a culture that objectifies and commodifies them.[16]

Girlhood and the Catholic Church

The triple bind is exacerbated in the context of the Catholic secondary school, where girls also have to deal with the Roman Catholic Church's official theological understanding of what it means to be a woman, an understanding that is rooted in a complementary dualism.[17] This

---

16 Hinshaw, *The Triple Bind*, 107.

17 See, for example, John Paul II, *Original Unity of Man and Woman: Catechesis on the Book of Genesis* (Boston: Daughters of St. Paul, 1981); John Paul II, *Man and Woman He Created Them: A Theology of the Body*, trans. Michael Waldstein (Boston: Pauline Books & Media, 2006). For a fuller description of complementary dualism and its critique by feminist theologians, see Gonzalez, *Created in God's Image*, 112–116; Johnson, *She Who Is*, 22–28.

approach posits that, while both men and women are created in the image of God, there are only two ways of being human and these ways of being human are designed by God to complement each other.[18] For women and girls, this means that their primary vocation is to motherhood and the nurturing and care of others. It also means that they are excluded from ordination and, therefore, from most positions of authority and leadership in the institutional Church.

In many ways, the experiences of girls in the Catholic Church reinforce the messages that they receive from the culture in the form of the triple bind. They are told that they must excel at femininity and caring for others, like the Virgin Mary or St. Therese of the Little Flower or Mother Theresa; they are told that this femininity is what women are created by God to do. At the same time, they are presented with conflicting messages about their adult roles in the Church. They can exercise leadership in the corporate world, but not in the Church; they can help and heal others as doctors, but not as priests.[19] And, finally, the third aspect of the triple bind—that girls must meet unrealistic standards of beauty—goes essentially unchallenged by the Church. The messages that girls receive from the Church not only implicitly support the message of the triple bind, they also reinforce the pressure to be perfect. The Church's saints are meant to be role models of faith; however, they are often presented to adolescent girls as models of perfection—perfectly holy, perfectly virgin, perfectly womanly. This can serve to reinforce for

---

18 In addition to locking women into a single prescribed notion of womanhood, this complementary dualism excludes any expressions of gender identity and/or sexual orientation that does not neatly fit into these definitions of masculinity and femininity. In a complementary dualism, there are only two sexes, with gender identity inextricably tied to biological sex; these two sexes exist to complement each other, initially in sexual intercourse, but extending to all areas of family and social life.

19 The young female editors of a book about young Catholic women put it this way: "Vocation can be a tricky thing for young Catholic women. In our lives outside the church, we have more career opportunities than Catholic women before us—and we expect that same expanse of opportunity in our church lives. . . . We seek active roles in our faith communities. [We] attend seminary with laymen and priests-in-training, ever aware that we are unable to answer calls to ordained priesthood." Kate Dugan and Jennifer Owens, "Introduction," in *From the Pews in the Back: Young Women and Catholicism*, ed. Kate Dugan and Jennifer Owens (Collegeville, MN: Liturgical Press, 2009), xxii..

girls that to be a faithful Catholic woman is also to be perfect and that to fall short of that perfection is to fail at being a Catholic woman.

Theology teachers in Catholic schools spoke about this tension between the Catholic Church's official theological anthropology and its effect on the girls in their care. Mia complained in particular about the ways that female saints are deployed as models of perfection. As an example, she described the ways that St. Maria Goretti—who, at age eleven forgave the young man who tried to rape her before dying of wounds inflicted in the attempted rape[20]—is held up for adolescent girls as a model of chastity and forgiveness. Viewed through the lens of the triple bind, this story reinforces the obligation of girls to manage their own sexuality, the sexual behavior of men and boys, and to smooth over any ruffled feathers in the process. It also reinforces the Church's expectation that femininity requires an orientation toward the care of others, as Maria provided forgiveness and mercy to her attacker. While the Church is clear that rape is sinful, this story blurs the boundaries of responsibility in Maria's attempted rape. As theology teacher Mia puts it, "stories like this make it so much harder for us to counter that perfect femininity model of the Church and to encourage girls to resist and report sexual harassment and assault. When the emphasis is on forgiving a rapist, girls can lose track of the need to also hold perpetrators accountable for their actions."

Feminist Perspectives on Defining Sin

In the Roman Catholic theological and pastoral tradition, there are many ways of defining what makes an individual's action sinful. Some of these definitions, especially when viewed through the lens of feminist critiques of Christian language about sin, are helpful for thinking about adolescent girls and mistake-making, while others reinforce the patriarchal culture of the triple bind and do not do anything to help adolescent girls understand their errors, whether sinful or not.

---

20 For more information on Maria Goretti, see, for example, "Maria Goretti," Wikipedia, accessed June 26, 2024, https://en.wikipedia.org/wiki/Maria_Goretti; "St. Maria Goretti," *Catholic News Agency*, accessed June 26, 2024, https://www.catholic-newsagency.com/saint/st-maria-goretti-530.

Feminist theologians interrogate Catholic (although not just Catholic) definitions of sin, with an eye toward the ways that the Church's rhetoric of sin can either reinforce the oppression of women and girls in a patriarchal context, such as that described above in the triple bind, or participate in the liberation of women and girls. Theologian Valerie Saiving's now classic article critiquing the traditional language of sin as pride (and the solution to this sin as self-effacing care for others) reveals the ways that the theological tradition has tended to define sin based primarily on the experiences of men.[21] And, as feminist theologian Rachel Sophia Baard argues, these definitions of sin do not merely exclude women's experiences, the doctrines themselves are sinful because they participate in the oppression of women.[22] In other words, in our patriarchal culture, the message that women need to become more holy by cultivating *more* self-sacrificial love for others only reinforces patriarchal expectations. When women are socialized to prioritize relationships and caring for others, they can lose themselves in a self-negating service of others. For adolescent girls, who are caught in the cross-pressures of the triple bind, this traditional messaging about sin reinforces the expectation that girls will excel at the "girl stuff"—the forming and maintaining of relationships—while, at the same time, not being too prideful of their success in the "boy stuff"—competing and achieving in school and career. In my interviews, John, an Asian American theology teacher at an all-girls' Catholic school, commented on the staying power of this definition of sin as pride and its effect on girls. He said, "Even here at an all-girls' school, where we are consciously trying to boost the self-esteem of girls, we struggle with this narrative of pride as sinful. Girls really resist taking pride in their accomplishments, often saying that they don't want to draw attention away from others, that their accomplishments are 'not a big deal.'"

---

21 Valerie Saiving, "The Human Situation: A Feminine View," in *Womanspirit Rising: A Feminist Reader in Religion*, ed. Carol P. Christ and Judith Plaskow (San Francisco: Harper & Row, 1979). Originally published in the *Journal of Religion* 40 (April 1960). The rooting of sin in pride can be traced to Augustine's discussion of sin as replacing the love of God with the love of self.
22 Rachel Sophia Baard, *Sexism and Sin-Talk: Feminist Conversations on the Human Condition* (Louisville, KY: Westminster John Knox Press, 2019), 61.

Other definitions of sin also fall into this same trap of reinforcing a patriarchal culture and furthering the oppression of women and girls. For example, sin is often defined as missing the mark, a deviation from what is good and right or from what God expects. For women and, especially, for girls, this definition of sin reinforces the sexist expectations of the triple bind. It fails to account for any intentionality in missing the mark. There is a difference between deliberately aiming away from the target and aiming for the target but not hitting it. The former may clearly be sin, but the latter may merely be a mistake or even an accident. The role of intentionality in sin is lost in a definition of sin as missing the mark. All efforts that are less than center of the target are imperfect and, therefore, sin.

This definition of sin fails girls in particular because expectations of perfection are embedded in the triple bind. The definition tends to treat, at least in the popular imagination, imperfection as sinful. Even a small missing of the mark—a small mistake—is understood as sin. Francine, a white campus minister, noted this tendency to count imperfection as sinful among the girls she works with. "I really see how girls don't differentiate between small mistakes and big mistakes, between messing something up by accident and intentionally screwing things up, between minor sins and major sins. Combine this with a sense of perfectionism and girls seem to blow their mistakes and minor sins out of proportion."

The Church's tradition of defining sin as a violation of relationships is a bit more ambiguous when it comes to how this rhetoric can affect women and girls. This definition can both reinforce the oppression of women and girls and it can provide a healthier way of thinking about sin and mistake-making. For women and girls, the danger of defining sin as a breakdown of relationships lies in the complementary dualism that is at the root of official Roman Catholic theological anthropology. This understanding of what it means to be female prioritizes the formation and nurturing of relationships as the defining characteristic of women's moral decision-making processes. Some of the early work by feminist scholars on questions of sin and moral decision-making still reflect this complementary dualism, even as they critique the focus on men and men's experiences. For example, Saiving named self-effacement as the primary sin of women as opposed to pride as the primary sin of men. Psychologist Carol Gilligan named an ethic of care as the primary way in which women and girls make moral decisions as opposed to a justice-oriented decision-making process as more characteristic of men.[23]

While Saiving and Gilligan are both helpful in naming the experiences of women, there is a danger that these perspectives are not seen as simply descriptive of the experiences of some (even many) women, but that they become prescriptive of how women should understand themselves. In other words, if women are socialized to prioritize relationships and if sin is a violation of relationships, it stands to reason that women are held to higher standards in regard to the formation and maintenance of relationships. And they bear more blame when relationships fail.

My interviewees reflected on this aspect of defining sin as a violation of relationships. Elizabeth, a white theology teacher, reflected on a conversation she had with a student in which this girl expressed her frustrations that she was expected to be the expert in all of her relationships, especially with boys. Elizabeth recalls:

> This student definitely felt like her relationships were her responsibility and, if they ran into trouble, it was her job to fix it. And, if the relationship failed, it was her fault. She said that, in a recent breakup, she felt like she was to blame even though the boy initiated the breakup. It is so hard to get girls, *this* girl, to see how relationships need to be two-way streets and they are not solely responsible for them.

Andrew, a priest and campus minister, echoed this saying, "These girls have so much on their plates; and then they take on so much more responsibility because of the ways we have made women think that the job of caring is a job for women."

---

23 Carol Gilligan, *In a Different Voice: Psychological Theory and Women's Development* (Cambridge, MA: Harvard University Press, 1982), 22. To be clear, Gilligan does not claim that only women use an ethic of care in their moral decision-making nor does she claim that the ethic of care is the only method of moral decision-making that women use. Rather, she identifies this ethic of care as more characteristic of women and an ethic of justice as more characteristic of men, although both men and women can and do use both approaches.

On the other hand, the turn in feminist theology in the twentieth century to the notion of relationality in God and humanity finds a deep resonance with the definition of sin as the breaking of relationships. Combined with the Catholic tendency to categorize sins as either mortal (very serious) or venial (less serious), a focus on relationality is helpful for thinking about girls, sin, and mistake-making.

For feminist theologians, focusing on relationality in theological anthropology highlights the relational nature of God as Trinity. God is overflowing love, expressed within Godself in a dance of interrelationships and expressed in God's loving creation of a human creature oriented toward relationship with God, others, and self. Relationality, rooted in love and justice, becomes a defining characteristic both of God and of all of humanity. Rooting a theological anthropology in relationality does several crucial things: it provides a solid foundation for a theological anthropology that grounds the full and flourishing humanity of women and girls (and, indeed, all humans) in our understandings of who God is; it recognizes the experiences of women and girls (who are most likely to be socialized for relationality) without making this relationality the exclusive or primary preserve of women; and it helps to put sin and mistake-making into a relational context without reinforcing the sexist expectations of the triple bind.

A Nuanced Relationality for Girls

Focusing on an understanding of sin as a violation of relationships helps put mistake-making and sin into a context that acknowledges the importance of relationships for adolescent girls and helps girls to resist some of the toxicity of the patriarchal culture through the triple bind. An understanding of sin as a breakdown of relationships means that, because humanity is created by God for relationship with God, others, and self, being relational is a part of what it means to be human.[24]

---

24 It is important to note, however, that some theologians, especially theologians focusing on disability, have pushed back on this notion of relationality being a defining characteristic of humanity, particularly the idea of relationality being the *sole* defining characteristic of humanity. Just as the focus of classical theological anthropology on rationality as the standard for humanity led male theologians to exclude women and others deemed "less rational" from their definition of full humanity, so to

Rooting relationality in our understandings of who God is can accomplish two goals. First, it removes responsibility for the creation and maintenance of relationships from women and girls. If God is relational, then everyone, regardless of gender identity, is called to relationship with God and others and everyone is responsible for the relationships they form. It gives those who work with girls, like counselor Suzanne, the opportunity to guide girls through the process of evaluating their relationships and their responsibilities to those relationships. Suzanne points out that

> because relationships are so important to girls—both because of their developmental stage and because of the ways that society has told them it is—this focus on God's relationality means that we can help them see that this is a fundamental human quality, not something that is unique to their experiences as girls. That it is okay to let others take up some of the responsibility for the relationships.

And, in response to theology teacher Elizabeth's lament above, it helps us to talk about the mutuality and shared responsibility that each person in a relationship has to the others in the relationship and for the maintenance of that relationship.

Within this understanding of sin as the breakdown of relationships with God, others, and self, the Catholic categorization of mortal and venial sins is useful in the moral formation of adolescent girls and for making the distinction between sin and mistake-making. For Catholics, a mortal sin is a very serious sin that *breaks* a relationship that one has with God, others, or self. A mortal sin is considered serious because, to some degree, the underlying purpose of the sinful action is the breaking of the relationship.[25] Very serious sins, such as murder

---

a focus *only* on relationality can—intentionally or unintentionally—exclude those for whom expressing relationality is difficult, such as those with cognitive or developmental disabilities. For a helpful summary of this issue, see Lorraine Cuddeback-Gedeon, "Disability: Raising Challenges to Rationality and Embodiment in Theological Anthropology," in *T&T Clark Handbook of Theological Anthropology*, ed. Mary Ann Hinsdale and Stephen Okey (New York: Bloomsbury, 2021), 338–340.

25 Darlene Fozard Weaver, "Sin and the Subversion of Ethics: Why the Discourse of Sin Is Good for Theological Anthropology," in *The T&T Clark Handbook of Theological Anthropology*, ed. Hinsdale and Okey, 104. Weaver lays out the conditions that make a sin a mortal sin: "For a sin to qualify as mortal it must meet several conditions.

or rape, have at their core an intention to destroy a relationship. Venial sins, on the other hand, are less serious actions that *harm* or *hinder* our ability to form and maintain relationships with God, others, and self. Venial sins are the things that we do that pick away at a relationship, potentially harming it enough to break it. For example, one individual lie told to a loved one may be only a minor thing, hindering but not damaging the relationship; but, a continuous and accumulating pattern of lying to a loved one can break down that relationship.[26] But, importantly, what the idea of venial sins provides is a way of talking about sin that recognizes the reality of less serious sins. In other words, in naming some sins as venial, the Church is telling us that not every single thing that we do wrong rises to the level of breaking down a relationship with God, others, or self. Not everything is equally bad; this is not an all-or-nothing approach to understanding sin, where one is either perfectly holy or a depraved monster. There is a middle ground, where most of us exist, where we are not perfect at honoring our relationships, but most of the time the things that we do wrong will not necessarily break them.

For theology teachers Mia and Elizabeth, this distinction between mortal sins and venial sins is extremely helpful in their classroom discussions of moral decision-making and mistake-making. While most of their students come into their classrooms knowing the technical definitions of mortal and venial sins, it is only in the course of prolonged conversation about these terms, particularly in the context of real-life examples, that girls come to the realization that minor errors are not major sins. As Elizabeth puts it, "at some point, the lightbulb goes on for them and they realize that not everything is an equally big deal. Not everything is a make-or-break choice." Mia's comments reflect this as well: "The ability to talk with girls about gradations of 'wrong-ness' means that we can talk honestly about blame. Not everything that goes wrong is something that they should blame themselves for. Not everything is their fault. Sometimes mistakes just get made."

It must be undertaken with full knowledge (an agent must know it is a sin) and consent (an agent must choose to commit the sin anyway), and it must involve 'grave matter'" (104).

26 Michele Saracino, *Christian Anthropology: An Introduction to the Human Person* (New York: Paulist Press, 2015), 160; Weaver, "Sin and the Subversion of Ethics," 104.

For campus minister Andrew, the opportunity to talk about "gradations of wrong-ness" comes up in the context of the sacrament of reconciliation. He finds that he is often having conversations with girls about what "counts" as a sin and he is able to draw on the Church's distinctions as a way of talking about mistakes and the role that intentionality plays in distinguishing between a mistake and a sin. This also provides a way of delving into the girls' understandings of confession and of taking appropriate levels of responsibility for one's actions. Andrew recounts his own realization that the ways that girls and women are shaped by society and the Church's teachings to prioritize relationships and to act out of an ethic of care means that he (and, indeed, all ministers) needs to think more carefully about what we are naming as sin and what we mean when we invite girls to confess to mistakes. He says that he routinely finds himself in conversations with girls who were conflating sinning and mistake-making and, more worryingly, trying to take responsibility for things that were not their fault. As he describes it,

> I see girls confess to very minor transgressions, like forgetting to return a text message or not returning a borrowed book on time. Unintentional mistakes. Nothing that should occupy their consciences excessively. And they were dwelling on these things, thinking that they were the most serious thing, something that would jeopardize their relationship with God. While it was a reminder to me of how girls are pressured to be perfect even in their relationships, it was also a chance to talk with these girls about mistakes. And how a mistake is not a sin. At worst, it might be something venial, but probably not even that "bad."

> I also talk with girls who have so internalized the pressure to take responsibility for the creation and maintenance of relationships that they take the blame for things that are clearly not their fault. Sometimes it's a minor thing—the girl blames herself for a friend's decision to do something wrong, for not successfully talking the friend out of it. But I get really worried when girls tell me about blaming themselves for abusive behavior from romantic partners. Everything from the girl who blames herself for a boyfriend's bad mood to the girl who thinks that her sexual assault is her fault. I blame our cultural shift of responsibility for relationships for girls who blame themselves for rape and assault and harassment. The Church does these girls a grave disservice in its rhetoric around sin and blame.

Talking with Girls about Mistakes and Sin

Since girls are navigating these tensions—the expectations of the triple bind, between sin and mistake, between blame-taking and responsibility-taking—they need the adults in their lives to engage them in conversation. Girls need adults who know them and can guide them in seeing these tensions and contradictions in the culture and in our theologies. Indeed, teachers, ministers, and other professionals working with girls in Catholic schools already have many ideas and strategies for countering the cultural messages and the theological misunderstandings that girls may experience.[27] Gathering these strategies around educational philosopher Elliot Eisner's notion of the three curricula found in schools is helpful for organizing insights for teaching girls about sin and mistake-making. First, for Eisner, the explicit curriculum is what a school intentionally teaches; this is usually found in the textbooks, curriculum plans, and course sequencing of a school. The explicit curriculum is what we teach through our formal instruction. Second, the implicit curriculum is what a school teaches through its day-to-day life—in its discipline policies, extracurricular activities, school climate, and so on. The implicit curriculum is what we teach through what we do. And, third, the null curriculum is what a school teaches through what it excludes from the explicit and implicit curricula; it is, for example, what we teach about sexism and misogyny when we ignore the sexual harassment that girls experience in the hallways. The null curriculum is what we teach by what we refuse or neglect to teach.[28]

Explicit curricula fail to adequately address the distinction between mistakes and sins in a way that enables adolescent girls to navigate the expectations put on them by culture and Church about female

---

27 What my interviewees suggest is, obviously, not an exhaustive list of strategies; rather, it reflects their experiences of exploring these issues with adolescent girls. It should be noted that it was in the context of our interview conversations that some of the connections between the toxicity of contemporary culture, the Church's rhetoric on sin, and the need to distinguish between sin and mistake were made in the thinking of these educators. In these cases, the interview conversations themselves prompted fresh theological reflection and pedagogical responses.

28 Elliott Eisner, *The Educational Imagination: On the Design and Evaluation of School Programs*, 3rd ed. (New York: Pearson, 2001), 87–107.

responsibility for relationships. John, for example, noted that, while the Church's model of gender complementarity is its official theological understanding of the relationship between femaleness and maleness, gender complementarity is not covered in any of the textbooks his school uses. The concept also does not easily fit into the scope and sequence plan that was approved by the United States Conference of Catholic Bishops.[29] In fact, John suggests that gender complementarity is part of the null curriculum instead of the explicit curriculum. "For all our rhetoric in girls' schools about female empowerment, we sometimes fail to talk about the ways that the Church's own teaching disempowers them. It just runs in the background without much conscious reflection." Thinking a bit more, he added: "Actually, it [gender complementarity] shows up most obviously in campus ministry, when only a priest can do certain things. But it's also there in our language about acceptable behavior at things like dances, about how it's the girl's responsibility to dress in a certain way and to act in a certain way." For John, this prompted a decision to seek out ways to talk with girls about gender complementarity in his theology classrooms, supplementing the explicit curriculum.

Similarly, reflecting on her course on moral decision-making, Elizabeth noted that she does not explicitly discuss mistakes in her classes.

> We talk about sin and even about mortal and venial sin; but, given the challenges of our world right now, we spend way more time on social sin. Which is good, of course. But I think I need to include more on moral discernment of what actually makes a sin sinful. If my girls think that things are sinful when they are just mistakes, then I think I need to do a better job of exploring that with them. So that they can figure out for themselves when something is a mistake. When they can just apologize for their mistake and move on.

Suzanne, the school counselor, suggested that including an explicit discussion of the societal pressures put on girls would be a good way to talk about the toxicity of perfectionism. She went on:

---

29 United States Conference of Catholic Bishops, *Doctrinal Elements of a Curriculum Framework for the Development of Catechetical Materials for Young People of High School Age* (Washington, DC: United States Conference of Catholic Bishops, 2008).

Actually, I think that needs to be a school-wide conversation with faculty. We all are aware of how perfectionism in girls can be paralyzing and disruptive; but we also all add to their search for the perfect—the perfect grade, the lead role, the captaincy of the team, getting into Harvard, and so on. We need to explore ways to back off that language of the perfect so we aren't reinforcing what the culture is telling them. This would go a long way to helping them stop catastrophizing their mistakes.

Most schools tend to have gaps in the explicit curriculum around questions of sin and mistake-making. Schools are leaving to the null curriculum things that need to be included in the explicit. By not talking about things like gender complementarity, mistake-making, and perfectionism, they are allowing the unwritten messages of the culture (such as the triple bind) and the Church (as in its theological anthropology) to teach students things that the schools do not actually want to teach.

In addition, the implicit curricula of Catholic schools reinforce these ideas. Mia, a theology teacher, pointed to her school's discipline policies. For example, she said, "we have a zero-tolerance policy for certain things like drugs and such. But I know there've been kids caught up and severely punished because of a mistake. Not to say that mistakes don't have consequences. But do we have a way of tempering the consequences to fit the mistake?" Elizabeth, on the other hand, shared an example of a way that her school avoids punishing a mistake. There, if a student becomes pregnant, the school's policy is that the girl remains in school and that the school will support the girl in continuing her pregnancy, assisting with childcare, and providing supportive services. As Elizabeth put it:

> By saying that one mistake doesn't have to derail your whole high school career and your future, we are trying to model to girls how love and community can work. While part of the impetus is in line with Church teaching on abortion, to make it possible for pregnant students to choose not to have an abortion, the policy also teaches girls that problems have solutions. That we can work with you to help you find a way through after you've done something.

Andrew, at his school, says that, as a priest, he tries to be very aware of the ways that the implicit curriculum—especially as it is played out in retreats and liturgies, in Christian service programs, and in the campus ministry office—can counter the cultural pressures and Church rhetoric about mistakes and perfectionism. In particular, he noted that Christian service programs could be used to effectively teach about mistakes and what he called incompleteness.

> Doing service often means doing something outside your comfort zone, doing something new. And doing something new means making mistakes and learning from them. Seeing mistakes as learning opportunities rather than problems. And, because our service is never going to be enough to solve the problems of poverty or homelessness, by its very nature, it shows that the work is always incomplete. And we can embrace that incompleteness. We make our contribution to the effort and allow others to contribute as well; we have to let go of completing the task, of being graded on it, of doing it perfectly.

Moving forward, Andrew said that he wants to narrate that incompleteness as a good thing when he is working with students at service sites. "We can't assume that they will figure it out on their own; we need to show them the mistakes and the incompleteness and we need to tell them why these are okay."

These experienced educators, reflecting on the adolescent girls in their care in their Catholic schools, suggest that the way to help girls navigate the cross-pressures of the triple bind and to better understand the ambiguities of the Church's teachings on sinning and mistake-making is to make these ideas explicit for them. They want to add critical conversations to the formal curricular goals and materials, to use the implicit curriculum to reinforce a more empowering vision for flourishing for adolescent girls, and to make explicit the things that have been relegated to the null curriculum. Teachers everywhere want the best for their students; these teachers see that talking with girls about mistake-making can be a part of equipping them for flourishing.

Adolescent girls in Catholic schools need help navigating the cross-pressures of the triple bind so that they can better understand the ambiguities of the Church's teachings on sinning and mistake-making. The challenge, of course, is finding ways to incorporate this learning into the life of the Catholic school so that girls can engage in the kinds of critical conversations that will help them see the triple bind, understand the nuances of a feminist approach to sin, and know that much of what they think is sinful is, in fact, merely a mistake from which they can learn. Girls need all of the adults in their lives—and particularly the teachers in their Catholic schools—to be on their side, to see their struggles and vulnerabilities, and to embrace their imperfections. To know that God already loves them, even in the messiness of growing up in the twenty-first century.

CHAPTER TWO

Mistake and Sin in Adolescent Sexuality

Emily S. Kahm

For adolescents, particularly for those raised in more conservative Christian traditions in the United States, mistake and sin are not just predominant ways to frame sexual experiences. They are nearly the *only* ways to acknowledge adolescent sexual expression.[1] In many Christian contexts, effectively all adolescent experiences of sexuality—whether solo or partnered, safe or unsafe, consensual or nonconsensual—are painted with the same negative brushstrokes. This approach not only loses each experience's individual granularity and specificity, but potentially discourages young people from critically thinking about their sexual decisions. If everything is a sin, or at least a mistake, then there is little value in differentiating between the types of risk involved or seeking a nuanced understanding of one's own desires. This negativity can also create confusion or cognitive dissonance for those in the Catholic tradition, which explicitly teaches that sexuality—the desire for loving and intimate human connection—is fundamentally good and an intrinsic part of all human persons.

This chapter will primarily explore the experiences of one specific group of young people—young adult women who were raised Catholic,

---

1 Here and throughout, I use the phrases "sexual expression" or "having sexual experiences" rather than "having sex" because "having sex" is oft-associated with penile–vaginal intercourse and thus is overly restrictive. "Being sexually expressive" can include acts that are less clearly rule-bound or heteronormative, such as mutual masturbation, oral or anal sex, sexting or sexually explicit video chatting, and so on, as all of these may be ways that adolescents explore or experiment with their sexuality.

reflecting on their adolescent[2] sexuality education and experiences—to examine their recollections of this mistake/sin framing, and to seek their wisdom on whether there are ways to frame being an adolescent with sexual feelings and drives that is not associated with negativity. Their voices will also be put into conversation with other relevant social scientific research. After reviewing the overarching context of the United States[3] when it comes to sexuality education and sexual activity among adolescents, we will turn to the voices of young adult women I interviewed about their sexuality education experiences while growing up Catholic, where three consistent themes arose: first, that parents are fearful about discussing sex openly; second, that adolescents want more guidance and information than they receive; and third, that all forms of "being sexual" as an adolescent are framed as mistakes by their parents and other adults. We will then explore how the framework of "mistake-making" and allowing young people to be fearful about sexuality can itself be a mistake on the part of parents and trusted adults when accompanying adolescents through their years of sexual nascence, and how to move forward from this framework toward a place of nuance and empowerment.

Adolescents and Sex in the United States

In focusing on the US context of sexuality and adolescence, few will be surprised to hear that the prevailing cultures are often contradictory.[4]

---

2 Here and throughout, "adolescents" will refer broadly to an age range roughly from eleven or twelve years old through the late teens. The specific age is less important than the experiences of undergoing puberty, or being surrounded by peers undergoing puberty, and the awakening of critical thought.

3 For this chapter, my focus will primarily be on US Catholicism with occasional references to Evangelicalism due to the focus of my research. Some themes will apply to other branches or denominations of Christianity, while others may not fit. Other religious traditions, even those regarded as "traditional" or "conservative," will explore morals around sexuality in distinct ways; for further reading, see Danya Ruttenberg, ed., *The Passionate Torah: Sex and Judaism* (New York: New York University Press, 2009); Yvonne Yazbeck Haddad, Jane I. Smith, and Kathleen M. Moore, *Muslim Women in America: The Challenge of Islamic Identity Today* (New York: Oxford University Press, 2006).

4 Given the US history of white supremacy and its present as a still white-dominated and white-domineering culture, there are many additional layers to how

US media is suffused with sexual content, especially in advertising, but, as a Christian-majority country, officially promoted sexual norms tend to be conservative. Catholicism, as the largest single denomination, as well as the various strands of Evangelicalism, promote a theology that states that most forms of sexual activity are only licit in heterosexual marriage. The broader "purity culture" movement, originating in Evangelicalism and sometimes echoed in conservative Catholicism, went farther with these expectations in the late 1990s, promoting a cessation of romantic dating (replaced by a parentally approved "courtship" system), and some writers went so far as to valorize the idea that one's first kiss should be at the altar on one's wedding day.[5]

Formal sexuality education in the United States is similarly inconsistent. The National Conference of State Legislatures reports that only twenty-two states out of fifty require sexuality education in public schools to be medically accurate and only thirty of fifty require sexuality education in any form.[6] "Abstinence-only" sexuality education was given major funding in the Clinton era and remains dominant—this form of sexuality education emphasizes that full abstinence from all forms of sexual activity until marriage is the only sure way to avoid unintended pregnancy and sexually transmitted infections—and typically does not include any information about contraception or STI

sexual cultures have sought to demean BIPOC communities in particular, such as the over-sexualizing of Black bodies. For further reading, see Sabrina Strings, *Fearing the Black Body: The Racial Origins of Fat Phobia* (New York: New York University Press, 2019).

5 This norm is often traced back to Evangelical Joshua Harris's series of purity books, beginning with *I Kissed Dating Goodbye* in 1997, though he was not the only source. Harris has since disavowed his books and left affiliation with Christianity. A series on TLC called *Virgin Diaries*, beginning in 2011, highlighted this practice as it featured stories of some young adults who had chosen for religious reasons to remain virgins until marriage, including "saving" their first kiss for the show, which was filmed and broadcasted for the series. This is part of a broader trend of back-and-forth-ing between more permissive and more restrictive sexual norms in the United States. See Kristi L. Slominski, *Teaching Moral Sex: A History of Religion and Sex Education in the United States* (New York: Oxford University Press, 2021), which goes into depth regarding this history. See also Joshua Harris, *I Kissed Dating Goodbye* (Sisters, OR: Multnomah Books, 2003).

6 National Conference of State Legislatures, "State Policies on Sex Education in Schools," National Conference of State Legislatures, October 1, 2020, https://www. ncsl.org/research/health/state-policies-on-sex-education-in-schools.aspx.

prophylaxis beyond the failure rates of various methods. Put differently, all adolescent sexual contact is framed as a mistake with potentially dire consequences. This type of sexuality education also usually excludes any discussion of sexual orientations beyond heterosexuality, and gender identifications beyond cisgender. Depending upon the state, district, funding, and parental involvement, the "required" sexuality education could take place in fourth grade as part of a unit on puberty, in high school as part a health science or gym class, or not at all. Religious schools are generally exempt from sexuality education requirements stipulated by the state; these schools may use their own curricula, integrate sexuality education into religion classes, or decline to provide sexuality education at all, and this once again can vary from school to school.

For all this lack of consistency in sexuality education, there is a marked level of consistency in rates of adolescent sexual experience—teens and adolescents are having sex, with the CDC's most recent report estimating that 30 percent of all US high school students have ever had sex, showing a small decrease over the decade.[7] This data, however, focuses primarily on heterosexual penetrative intercourse, and thus sexual acts like oral sex, mutual masturbation, video/text-based sexual interactions, and many or most homosexual experiences would be excluded; one can safely imagine that the numbers of adolescents who have been sexually active in these non-intercourse ways would be higher.

With this context in mind, it should not be surprising that adolescents are anxious and uncertain about how to direct their burgeoning sexual drives; they may fear being too sexually inexperienced by broad cultural standards, but "impure" by their religious standards. Nearly any decision they can make will be regarded as a mistake by some significant group.

---

7 Centers for Disease Control and Prevention, Division of Adolescent and School Health, "Youth Risk Behavior Survey Data Summary & Trends Report: 2011–2021," accessed June 27, 2024, https://www.cdc.gov/healthyyouth/data/yrbs/pdf/YRBS_Data-Summary-Trends_Report2023_508.pdf.

Learning from Adolescent Experiences

Ideally, to better understand the sexual experiences of adolescents and their internalization of a mistake/sin framing, one would speak directly to adolescents. In practicality, though, this can be difficult, both in terms of ensuring full and uninfluenced consent from both adolescents and their parents to broach these topics, and because younger adolescents may not have practiced the sort of critical self-reflection and explanation skills that are needed for the depth of qualitative research.

This chapter, then, focuses on young adult women (aged 18–25) reflecting back on their adolescent experiences with the additional knowledge and critical lenses that come from more years and more diverse lives.[8] All these women had been raised Catholic, but only about half continued to identify with the Catholic faith into young adulthood. As young adults, these women were better situated to imagine the sorts of sexuality education that could have more positively prepared them for their romantic and sexual explorations in their fledging years. Our conversations focused on their religious upbringing and how they saw the sexuality education of their adolescence—especially that provided in religious contexts—affecting the way they had learned to make decisions about sex and sexuality in young adulthood. These women ranged from highly conservative Catholic to militantly atheist, with some having transitioned to Protestant traditions and others staying nominally affiliated with the Catholic tradition they were raised in while not practicing. Their sexuality education experiences were similarly diverse, as were the ways they were living into their sexual selves in young adulthood. Their stories form the basis for the key moments and takeaways discussed below.

---

8 These interviews were part of a larger project on sexuality education and formation experiences in young adult women who were raised Catholic, and how they believed their educational experiences had prepared them (or failed to prepare them) for sexual decision-making in young adulthood. This project was approved by the Institutional Review Board at the University of Denver on May 14, 2015. Emily Kahm, "Catholic Girls All Grown Up: A Practical Theological Exploration of Sexuality Formation in Young Adult Women" (Iliff School of Theology and the University of Denver, 2017), https://digitalcommons.du.edu/etd/1288.

Parents and the Sex Talk

> In 4th grade, my mom handed me a book and then said, "If you have
> any questions, ask."
>
> —COREY[9] (20), NO RELIGIOUS AFFILIATION

Corey sums up a remarkably common experience for adolescents when it comes to learning about sex and sexuality—a rushed, or awkward, or detached single encounter with a parent[10] that came with no follow-up. While Corey's account is perhaps more abrupt than some others', parents often do not seem confident when addressing sex and sexuality with their adolescent children. This tendency is so common, in fact, that it functions as something of a trope in US sexuality education, with sitcoms playing the awkwardness of "the talk" for laughs[11] and researchers acknowledging that sexuality information coming from home is often incomplete and sometimes nonexistent.[12]

Of the young people who do hear directly from their parents about sex and sexuality, the experience is frequently far from positive. Some of this comes, understandably, from the awkwardness of the topic for both parties, but many talks were abbreviated to the point that young people felt they were being preemptively judged for having any interest in sexuality at all, or put on notice about the terrible consequences that would inevitably follow all sexual experiences. One twenty-year-old Catholic participant, Allison, described her sex-ed conversations with her mother as focused primarily on her virginity:

> Her favorite, favorite analogy is the present analogy. Like, you only give
> a gift once, you wouldn't want a gift to be given to you opened. Saying

---

9 All participant names are pseudonyms.

10 Here and throughout, "parent" can refer to biological parenting as well as parents through adoption, fostering or shorter-term care, and those who have stepped into parental mentoring roles, regardless of their biological relationship to the young person in question.

11 There is, in fact, a fairly robust page on the TV Tropes website on exactly this phenomenon; see "Sex Miseducation Class," TV Tropes, accessed June 27, 2024, https://tvtropes.org/pmwiki/pmwiki.php/Main/SexMiseducationClass.

12 Catherine Buni, "Let's (Not) Talk about Sex," *Boston Magazine*, April 5, 2022, https://www.bostonmagazine.com/education/2022/04/05/sex-education/.

so you save yourself for like marriage or whatever. . . . Even with boys, like, she was always really picky about [who] we were hanging out with.

While Allison had no problem with her mother's choice of analogy, the fact that she puts it in context with her mother's "pickiness" about the boys she hung out with indicates that this gift framework was associated with judgment and some fear that Allison might be too generous with her one "gift."

Allison had largely adopted her mother's philosophy about the importance of sexual purity. Recently, she had refused to kiss a boy and felt deep pride in this choice to not use her sexual capacity frivolously. However, other youths do not accept the norms their parents set in these conversations. Nora, a twenty-one-year-old agnostic, experienced a painful rift in her relationship with her parents when she left their traditionalist form of Catholicism. Conversations about sex were one of the first places she noticed the distinction between who she was and who her parents wanted her to be. "You knew that every question kind of had a value judgment attached to it. Like that was a good question or a bad question. And if you ask too many bad questions . . . probably wasn't a good sign for you!" Nora even later quipped that asking questions about sex was (hyperbolically) seen by her mother as a sign she must be "sleeping with the whole neighborhood!" Curiosity, in Nora's family, felt like a slippery slope into sinfulness.

Among my participants, there were few whose experiences learning about sex and sexuality from their parents were largely positive, and none who felt these parental interactions were fully adequate. This, again, echoes research literature that indicates parents may not address these topics at home at all. A 2010 report from the Centers from Disease Control and Prevention indicated that roughly one-third of teenage males and one-fifth of teenage females (between fifteen and seventeen) in the United States never spoke with their parents about certain sexual topics like declining sexual opportunities or how to use contraception.[13] A more recent survey conducted by OnePoll found that

---

13 Gladys Martinez, Abma Joyce, and Casey Copen, "Educating Teenagers about Sex in the United States: National Center for Health Statistics Data Brief," *Centers for Disease Control and Prevention*, Data Brief no. 44 (2010), https://doi.org/10.1037/e665512010-001.

out of 2,000 parents of children between the ages of five and eighteen, 21 percent do not plan to have a "sex talk" with their children at all.[14] As Rose, a nineteen-year-old convert to Evangelicalism put it, "I know some people really think it should be a parents' place, but at the same point, then you have parents like mine who kind of dance around it and they're like '. . . Okay, good, bye!'" For youth growing up in religious contexts, the awkwardness around the sex talk—if they ever got one to begin with—set the stage for unclear boundaries or expectations, thus increasing their anxiety that they would fail to live up to someone's standards, or make a mistake that they would not know how to handle.

Information That Adolescents Need

> In 8th grade, our religion class went a little bit more in depth and there was some kind of pamphlet that we got, and it had a couple holding hands on the beach on the front of it. It was a very cheesy thing, and it answered all those questions that you had. But they didn't talk to us about it. They just gave it to us. So I always was frustrated by that.
>
> —MELANIE (21), CATHOLIC

> [My Catholic abstinence book] never really explained why. It was just focused on, "This is what the church teaches. Sex is for procreation and unity," and that's the extent of it. It wasn't anything beyond that. So . . . it wasn't very helpful.
>
> —ISABELLA (21), CATHOLIC

The frustration represented by Melanie and Isabella demonstrates a consistent theme from these conversations—none of the opportunities these women had to learn more about sex and sexuality felt adequate. Whether they were missing useful information about dating and relationships, the "whys" behind stern moral recommendations, or a chance for meaningful dialogue, I spoke to no one who felt their education was full and complete. This certainly could speak to a broader adolescent tendency to be critical of adults without understanding the

---

14 OnePoll Research, "Six in 10 American Parents Were Raised Thinking Sex Was 'Taboo,'" March 2, 2022, https://www.onepoll.us/six-in-10-american-parents-were-raised-thinking-sex-was-taboo/.

complexity behind their decisions, and almost certainly resonates with a cultural perception that adults do not particularly like interacting with adolescents,[15] but the consistency of their discontent was notable across religious identities and levels of sexual experience.

When these participants were asked how they would approach sex and sexuality if they had a child of their own one day, they were enthusiastic about how differently they would handle sex ed. "I would try to like open up that dialogue, and say like 'You know, if you have questions, talk to me,'" asserted Jessica, a twenty-year-old Catholic. "'If ever you feel pressure, you can come talk to me.' And I think I would put less of an emphasis on kind of that black-and-white like 'Don't do this, don't do this, don't do this.'" Melanie echoed much the same sentiment when asked, saying, "I would probably try to talk to her [early] so she doesn't go to school and come home and be like 'What is this that you didn't tell me?'" Melanie was particularly concerned with establishing that baseline of trust with a future daughter so that she would be the first and most trusted resource, but also has an eye toward ensuring her hypothetical child wouldn't feel behind their peers or embarrassed about their lack of knowledge. This point is repeated by Lily, an eighteen-year-old Spiritualist, saying, "I want them to hear it from us first, rather than anywhere else. Instead of seeing stupid boys do stupid things . . ." Lily is here reflecting on her own experience of learning about oral sex from adolescent gossip and her own memory of being scandalized and shocked in a way she could not hide from her peers, which singled her out as being uninformed. This perspective helps highlight that adolescents want more information not only for their own ability to make good choices and avoid mistakes, but also because they are anxious to maintain whatever dignity they can in social spaces—ignorance about sexuality feels like vulnerability.

Other literature supports the idea that this sense of being underinformed and unfulfilled by the education on offer is a fairly common adolescent experience. A Harvard Graduate School of Education survey

---

15 Katherine Turpin provides a deeper exploration of the phenomenon of adult avoidance of working with adolescents; see Katherine Turpin, "A Cloud of Unknowing: Articulations of Identity and Faith in Younger Adolescents," *Sacred Spaces* 6 (2014): 117–142.

on sexuality education states that teens in the study wished they knew a lot more about true love and healthy relationships and wished their parents had talked with them about relationship issues like break-ups.[16] One can imagine that these relationship-oriented topics are often shunted aside in favor of biological information, but other resources indicated significant confusion about the physical aspects of sexuality as well, with one study finding that teens had little idea when a female would be fertile during her cycle.[17] The same study found some significant minorities of teens who are misinformed about the normality of bleeding during menstrual periods or who believed sex during pregnancy would be physically harmful. When participants were asked what they thought should be included in sexuality education, "Many indicated they wanted 'everything' included and 'nothing' excluded."[18] Despite the difficulty of articulating what, specifically, would be interesting or helpful to them, adolescents were determined that more was better than less.

Beyond Sexual Encounters as Mistakes

> They would give you a page of ideas about like how we're created in the image and likeness of God and blah blah blah blah blah and then the practical side of it was two sentences at the end. "So don't have sex outside of marriage."
>
> —JESSICA (22), CATHOLIC

Cognitive psychologists remind us that adolescents are still developing their conceptions of cause and effect and thus will not have a full sense of the potential consequences of their actions; this is an age caught between childlike impulsiveness and adult consideration. In the conversations I had, the dominant method of trying to make up for this developing ability seemed to be adults simply telling adolescents what

---

16 Harvard Graduate School of Education, "The Talk: How Adults Can Promote Young People's Healthy Relationships and Prevent Misogyny and Sexual Harassment," Making Caring Common Project, May 2017, https://tinyurl.com/mpc6ekdd, 2.
17 Gail S. Risch and Michael G. Lawler, "Sexuality Education and the Catholic Teenager: A Report," *Journal of Catholic Education* 7, no. 1 (September 2003): 59–60.
18 Risch and Lawler, "Sexuality Education and the Catholic Teenager," 64.

those outcomes will be and, thus, why they should not participate in risky behavior. However, in morally tricky topics, this can devolve into suggesting that the worst possible outcome is the most likely. One can easily call to mind antidrug campaigns that imply that a single use of an illicit substance produces addiction.[19] Similarly, negative outcomes are overemphasized in sexuality education, leading to young people who think condoms are entirely ineffective at pregnancy prevention because they have a failure rate, or even a student I once taught who believed that any sexual contact with a person who had HIV would result in contracting the virus and dying shortly thereafter. Overall, this produces an environment of high stakes and high anxiety for adolescents who are repeatedly told that any mistakes or missteps will have lifelong consequences.

This high-pressure environment was described at length by most of my participants. Rose, who came from a Catholic school environment, related this well:

> I can't even tell you how many times I've gotten scared because it's deeply embedded in me—"What if there's something wrong? What if I got pregnant? What if this happened, what if that happened?"—that I know my other friends who didn't go through Catholic schooling don't worry about.

Expressing similar stress was Bridget, a twenty-year-old conservative Catholic, who had made a hardline commitment to not having sex before marriage and never using birth control, but who also had a serious boyfriend. They had come to an unsteady, unspoken agreement that anything that wasn't penetrative intercourse was okay, and even so, "A lot of times I'm kind of upset with myself that this is what I'm doing, but on the other hand, it's life. So, whatever, sometimes I'm too tired to care. Too stressed out." Both Rose and Bridget seemed unable to make sexual decisions they were fully happy with, even after consideration and experimentation, due to the high-pressure expectations they had

---

19 Banyan Treatment Center, "Why Did the DARE Program Fail? Banyan Treatment Centers," September 29, 2021, https://www.banyantreatmentcenter.com/2021/09/29/dare-program-failure/.

been taught about what good sexuality looked like and the outcomes for those who failed to live up to that standard.

Furthermore, some of my participants experienced harm specifically *because* the high-anxiety environment perpetuated by their parents meant they could not access the information or resources they needed; they relied on sexual experimentation to answer their questions when they felt their parents would not. Willow, a twenty-two-year-old queer[20] agnostic, contracted herpes in her teens due to not knowing how to use prophylaxis; Corey, the twenty-year-old mentioned above, dealt with multiple pregnancy scares because she could not get birth control without going through her parents' insurance. She related her painful experiences to me about how, during each scare, she would begin to make panicked plans about who might be willing to house her when, as she assumed, her parents inevitably kicked her out of her home. Because all sexual encounters were framed as mistakes, these women had no knowledge about or access to harm reduction and safer sexual practices. The lack of nuance about the possible dangers of sexual exploration put them in more danger rather than less, even as their parents sought to protect them.

It can be helpful to remind young people who are highly motivated by pleasure-seeking that pleasure can come with downsides too, in hopes that they slowly widen their perspective and recognize a variety of possible outcomes from their actions. However, it is hard to argue that parents or teachers should want adolescents to be constantly fearful. There is also the issue of blowback once a young person realizes that adults are overemphasizing negative outcomes; this can read to an adolescent as if adults have been lying to them, and thus should not be trusted resources for significant information.[21]

Even more relatively progressive sexuality educators in the Catholic tradition, such as Bob Bartlett, interviewed for a *US Catholic* article on how to discuss sex with adolescents, trend toward the pathologizing of sexual desire and the inherent mistake-ness of all sexual activity. While Bartlett clearly acknowledges the reality that many teens are

---

20 Queer is the descriptor Willow chose for herself, referring to her perception of being outside the norm in both gender presentation and sexual orientation.
21 Banyan Treatment Center, "Why Did the DARE Program Fail?"

participating in partnered sexual activities and wants to help them learn from their experiences, the baseline assumption is that the experiences were negative or harmful. The article, while discussing better options for sexuality education in the Catholic tradition, explains that "[Bartlett] tries to help [teens] figure out for themselves what they were looking for in a sexual relationship and how they can fill that emotional need without sex."[22] Bartlett is then quoted saying that Jesus forgave sexual sins because "he knew [the sexually active persons] were looking for something good and went about it the wrong way."[23] In both cases, the assumption is that teenage or premarital sex is obviously bad, but that young people seek it out because they are unfulfilled. If they *were* emotionally balanced, Bartlett seems to suggest, they would not desire to have sex, or at least not struggle to remain abstinent despite their desires.

The impulse to look for underlying motivations for behavior, especially behavior that could be harmful, is important. However, the framework Bartlett presents suggests that teens who have sex must be missing something significant in their lives. Therefore, if an adolescent experiments with sexual activity, or even if they want to but do not have the opportunity, it can only be because there is something deeply wrong with them. Put less subtly, Bartlett's explanation for the root causes of teen sexual experimentation suggests that healthy teens simply do not have sex. Teens may hear this message and recognize the compassion that surrounds it, but it reinforces the same set of rules as more directly sex-negative education—a so-called good teen cannot be sexually active, and should suppress their sexual feelings. Sexual activity at this age is not just risky, but actively harmful, and even wanting to be sexually expressive is an indicator of being messed up. Bartlett, again laudably, promotes the need for adults to be compassionate listeners to adolescents who have been sexually active, but only in the service of damage control, saying that "Often teens who have made mistakes already are suffering from the emotional or physical damage and need guidance to get their life back on track."[24] The "back on track" language

---

22 Liz DeCarlo, "Intimate Conversations: How to Talk to Your Kids about Sex," *US Catholic*, November 3, 2018, https://uscatholic.org/articles/200811/intimate-conversations-how-to-talk-to-your-kids-about-sex/.
23 DeCarlo, "Intimate Conversations."
24 DeCarlo, "Intimate Conversations."

is particularly reminiscent of addiction language, and adds to the perception that sexual activity is only sought out by the broken.

We must never downplay the negative outcomes that *can* be the result of adolescent sexual activity. Adolescents can and do experience trauma resulting from nonconsensual[25] experiences, and they can and do contract sexually transmitted infections or experience unintended pregnancy. But if we must not assume the best—or even the neutrality—of these experiences, so too we must not always assume the worst. Some adolescents and teens do not regard their sexual experiences as negative, shameful, harmful, or scary, and it is oversimplifying for others to always rewrite those stories to fit the mistake narrative. Teens and adolescents are not fully adult, but they are capable of complex decision-making, and they should be given the space to name and describe their own experiences, though adults may need to put these descriptions in a bigger context. There is more to being sexual than mistakes.

Enjoying the Goodness of Sexuality

Ultimately, the high anxiety that comes from a consistent mistake framework around all sexual expression is aimed at a full cessation of sexual behavior. If teens are fearful of pregnancy or STIs or eternal damnation, they will suppress, or at least internalize, their sexual interests and desires until a more appropriate time. This strategy, however, runs counter to the more expansive understanding of sexuality promoted by the Catholic Church, which describes sexuality as:

> affect[ing] all aspects of the human person in the unity of his [sic] body and soul. It especially concerns affectivity, the capacity to love and procreate, and in a more general way the aptitude for forming bonds of communion with others. The fundamental drive towards relationship

---

25 This also includes what might be called "preconsensual" experiences, which in the United States are sexual experiences where one participant is below the legal age of consent—that is, they are assumed by their age and subsequent lack of experience and knowledge to be unable to meaningfully consent to sexual activity, especially with an older partner. Such legal distinctions can function as starting points to think more deeply about power differentials in sexual encounters and how they can muddle or invalidate consent.

and intimacy that undergirds all friendships as well as romantic pairings.[26]

Sexuality is not a sinful aspect of humanity. Sexuality is an inborn orientation toward connection. It is part of the broad spectrum of relating to others, and thus sexuality cannot and should not be suppressed.

Imagine telling an adolescent that having a good friend was inherently risky or a slippery slope toward life-altering mistakes. Given that friendship and romantic relationship are, according to the Church's definition of sexuality, coming from the same fundamental interest in being connected, it is surely confusing to adolescents to be told that this urge is important and good when labeled as friendship and worrisome when labeled as romantic. Many fully-fledged adults are familiar with how deeply intwined the two impulses can feel. To ask an adolescent to constrain their sexual self while still growing emotionally and relationally would be somewhat like asking them to get all the blue paint out of a can of purple paint. The paint is already mixed together, and the task feels impossible to the point of silliness. Yet many in the religious sphere still default to pathologizing sexual interest and expression in adolescents, framing sexual desire as a mistake rather than a normal aspect of personhood.

It is no wonder that adolescents can feel intense anxiety around sex and sexuality if these experiences cannot be distinguished from their desires to know and be known by others. For many young people, this frustration can become burdensome enough that they see their only option is to throw away the expectations they have been given and start from scratch, perhaps entirely without religious or adult guidance.

The true mistake in religious sexuality education is how parents, teachers, pastors, and other stakeholders allow the inherent goodness of sexuality to be obscured through a negative and fear-based framing. If Christians believe that sex and sexuality are sacred and God-given gifts, they should explain these experiences using joy and honor, not judgment and implicit threats.

However, correcting this trajectory is complicated. Many Christians believe that sexual exploration should be carefully considered and

---

26 Catholic Church, *Catechism of the Catholic Church*, 2nd ed. (Washington, DC: Libreria Editrice Vaticana, 2000), para. 2332.

postponed *because* of its sacrality. It is easy to worry that presenting sexuality as good and fun to adolescents will encourage them to explore it immediately in ways their growing bodies and brains may not be fully prepared for. Sexual exploration *does* come with risks, and most adolescents are not yet capable of making well-reasoned predictions about the potential positive and negative outcomes of their behaviors. What, then, are parents and educators to do?

Rather than trying to squelch adolescent sexual energy, Christian parents, educators, and other stakeholders might seek to imagine ways to help adolescents direct and enjoy that energy while avoiding risks they are unprepared for. This orientation could better serve adolescent development, and may actually achieve their desired outcomes of avoiding more risky behavior more effectively. Put differently, instead of constantly saying "no," adults should find ways to say "yes" to a young person's sexual growth, recalling that sexuality is the drive toward connection and intimacy in all forms, not just carnal forms. Adults should find ways to declare that there are many expressions of sexuality that are *not* mistakes.

What adults are ready to encourage will vary among Christian traditions and personal beliefs, but could include myriad ways to support adolescents in exploring this God-given human capacity.[27] A parent or trusted adult might encourage and support the intense friendships that often take root in adolescence, ensuring that young people have ample opportunities to be with people they like in shared hobbies, sleepovers, camps, and clubs, expressing curiosity rather than judgment when an adolescent cleaves strongly to a friend that they want to text, email, or connect with on social media seemingly all the time. Adults can directly encourage adolescents to seek friendships across genders, given that many (though certainly not all) young people will eventually seek out heterosexual romantic relationships; friendships are a wonderful

---

27 The Our Whole Lives series used by the United Church of Christ and Unitarian Universalist Association can be an excellent resource for comprehensive, medically accurate sexuality education information that is presented in a way to help students reflect on their own values and attitudes, including those informed by their religious beliefs. For more information about this series, see "Our Whole Lives: Lifespan Sexuality Education," Unitarian Universalist Association, accessed June 27, 2024, https://www.uua.org/re/owl.

starting point in practicing for deeper connection. It may be helpful to normalize crushes and flirtations without the teasing ("Oooh, you have a boyfriend?") or vague threatening ("You can't date until you're sixteen or else!") that can embarrass or shame a young person so they feel the need to hide their burgeoning interests.

Depending on the theology one is working from, parents may feel empowered to encourage their adolescent to masturbate as a way of enjoying and relieving sexual tension that has nearly no health or emotional risk factors,[28] and as a way of familiarizing themselves with their own body and feeling ownership of their sexual pleasure. Opening the conversation to masturbation also offers a context for discussing fantasizing, media depictions of what is considered sexually appealing, and pornography. Regardless of a parents' viewpoint on masturbation, they can encourage their adolescent to take good care of their body and to be highly aware of their bodily feelings. For example, parents can take an interest in a sports injury rather than telling adolescents to shrug it off. They can follow up by inquiring about how the injury feels for the adolescent throughout the healing process. Relatedly, adults can model consent practices by asking adolescents about what sorts of physical affection they are comfortable or uncomfortable with and respecting those boundaries, while also being clear that bodies do have touch needs and that it's good and right to enjoy embraces with friends, cuddling with pets, and affection from parents or siblings.

For adolescents who are already involved in romantic relationships, parents can be ready to express what they think some good physical options might include rather than resorting to vague platitudes ("Leave room for the Holy Spirit!"). If one feels that hand-holding, hugging, or kissing are pleasant ways of demonstrating affection at this age and stage, they can say so specifically and remind their young person that they do not have to try any act that they do not feel completely comfortable with. Parents can also encourage friendship and emotional intimacy over physical intimacy by offering shared public or group activities they can attend together, and allowing text message or social media interactions.

---

28 Jennifer Huizen, "Masturbation: The Positive and Negative Effects on the Brain," *Medical News Today*, October 27, 2020, https://www.medicalnewstoday.com/articles/masturbation-effects-on-brain.

Many adolescents can become deeply immersed in a specific media—books, TV shows, video games, anime, and so on—that help them reflect on who they are and want to be, and not infrequently are the source of fictional crushes or vicarious experiences of romance. It is important that adults do not trivialize these safe avenues to exploring real hopes and fears around attraction. Given that adolescents are oftentimes far more excited to discuss a series or fictional world they love than other topics, adults can both honor the importance of these obsessions and help their young person practice deeper thinking and verbal expression by showing interest and asking questions ("He *is* pretty cute! Does he have a good personality?"). Young people may express their enthusiasm (as well as other, more private feelings) in art, poetry, or fiction writing. Again, these are very safe outlets for sexual energy, and are avenues for self-expression and exploring wants and desires outwardly, which lays groundwork for self-advocacy and communicating desires and limits in friendships or romantic relationships later.

The Goodness of Mistakes

Making mistakes is a fully normal and human way of learning about oneself and one's environment. Adolescents, with their still-nascent abilities to imagine outcomes and effects from their actions, should be expected to make quite a lot of mistakes.[29] Mistakes should be understood relatively neutrally as things that can produce difficult outcomes but which are also simply learning experiences. With that in mind, mistakes and their fallout are best approached with aplomb and an eye toward safety and problem-solving rather than lecturing or shaming. Parents and adults who have refrained from judgmental language around relationships and sexuality will likely stand a better chance of their young person being willing to talk through a difficulty or mistake with them. Critically, this also provides groundwork for an adolescent to seek adult input on a situation in which they feel unsafe or for which they feel unprepared, or in circumstances that do require direct adult intervention.

---

29 So too should all adults. Mistakes are a normal part of navigating complex worlds, spaces, and relationships.

The difference between mistake and sin is important considering how adolescents experience decision-making. Sins, at least in Catholic contexts, are bad things that a person has done despite knowing they were wrong,[30] whereas mistakes might consist of the same act but without the foreknowledge that this act would be wrong. Adolescents are mentally just beginning the move from an external conscience (that's wrong because powerful people say it is) to an internal conscience (this is wrong because it doesn't align with my values)[31] and frequently experiment with things they have been told are bad to find out for themselves if the proffered warnings are true. This experimentation is not disobedience, or malice, or assholery. This is age-appropriate exploration and verification. Despite the incredible irritation that parents and adults will certainly feel when they have warned a young person that, for example, they will do poorly on their math test if they do not study, when their young person seems surprised and outraged at this patently obvious outcome, it is key that adults recall that the outcome was not obvious to the adolescent and that they are learning far more effectively from these consequences than they would ever learn from what someone tells them. In short, as so many adolescent parenting guides will echo, adults should do their best to avoid attributing negative motivations to adolescents who mess up. With this in mind, it is difficult to classify many adolescent missteps as sins. Adolescents are growing their capacity to figure out right from wrong for themselves, not just because someone told them so.

Embracing the Confusion

Romantic relationships and sexual expression are, indeed, intense and at times risky; it makes good sense that parents and religious educators would be anxious that adolescents do not wade too far into activities

---

30 More specifically, a serious sin must involve a grave matter and the person must consent to the sinful action freely and without coercion. See *Catechism of the Catholic Church*, para. 1857.

31 Developmental theologian James Fowler discusses this as the move from "conventional" faith to "individuative" faith; see James W. Fowler, *Stages of Faith: The Psychology of Human Development and the Quest for Meaning* (San Francisco: HarperOne, 1995), 179.

they are not mentally, physically, or emotionally prepared for. However, adults must be cautious to not pass along that anxiety to young people who are already plenty apprehensive about fitting into an increasingly complex social world.

In the years since completing my study of young adult women, I have become a mother of two and gained a far greater appreciation for the difficulties that my participants' parents faced in trying to address sex and sexuality in a complicated and sometimes dangerous world. While my children are years from puberty, I still wrestle daily with when to explain in detail the various ways that they could experience harm from, say, jumping on the couch, so that they understand the reasoning behind my instructions, and when to simply lay down a rule that they must follow or face consequences. There are no simple answers for raising children, regardless of age, and no good way to predict how they will remember the lessons a parent, teacher, or trusted adult tried to impart upon them.

Still, a trusted adage for dealing with toddlers seems to apply to adolescent sexual education: try not to say no to one thing without saying yes to something else. Redirect, offer options, let them know what they can do rather than only what they can't. Create boundaries, yes, but offer space within those boundaries for growth and exploration. This requires parents and other trusted adults to do their own work around sex and sexuality, to deal with any shame or confusion they have retained, and to acknowledge that their children are growing up into sexual people. None of this is easy, but when the outcome could be young adults who trust themselves, who have knowledge to keep themselves safe and confidence to express their desires, the work is worth it.

CHAPTER THREE

Christian Girlhood Books and Evangelical Culture

Jennifer Moe

Conservative evangelical Christian publishers offer books such as *Smart Girls, Smart Choices, Lies Young Women Believe and the Truth That Sets Them Free, Perfectly Unique, Dateable,* and *His Princess* to young Christian women with an emphasis on making good (or right or smart) choices during the formative years of adolescence. The implication is that making good choices will protect young women from devastation of all kinds because God will honor those good choices with good rewards. These titles encourage purity of thought, word, and deed, promote a socio-psycho-biological determinative understanding of gender, and enforce these themes using a particular biblical hermeneutic. Collectively, these themes encourage silencing of the self, denial of one's own desires, a pursuit of excellence that leaves no room for mistakes, and conformation to a patriarchal, heteronormative standard that makes no room for individuality.

Purity of Thought, Word, and Deed

One such book, *Smart Girls, Smart Choices: Avoiding the 10 Biggest Mistakes Young Women Make,* written by Megan Clinton, includes behaviors such as focusing too much on oneself and not focusing enough on God.[1] The author charges girls to rein in their feelings so they do

---

1 Megan Clinton, *Smart Girls, Smart Choices: Avoiding the 10 Biggest Mistakes Young Women Make* (Eugene, OR: Harvest House Publishers, 2010).

not make the mistake of being controlled by their emotions.[2] The book includes an anonymous quote stating, "Don't blindly trust your heart. It's too fragile. And besides, *it's not on the right side.*"[3] Clinton does not chastise girls for having emotions. She simply tells girls that the right thing to do is give those feelings over to God and to not act on them. A young woman in this chapter deftly reveals a sexist thread that runs throughout the book: "It's easy for me to be influenced way too much by how I feel. I'm learning that this can get us girls into big trouble sometimes."[4]

Being led astray by emotions is not just a mistake in these kinds of texts. It is a mistake particularly found in girls. These mistakes affect girls by causing them to listen to themselves and their own desires rather than trusting God, with the implication being that what a girl wants and what God wants must not be in alignment. Since God is a capital-H "He" and the books themselves are invested in gendered stereotypes about girls and women, it is not a stretch to presume that a male God knows what is best for girls and women and speaks to them through a patriarchal church and a Bible read through patriarchal eyes.

There is also heavy emphasis on dating and relationships that focuses on right or good choices and the maintaining of purity in young women's budding sexual identities. Justin Lookadoo and Hayley DiMarco make the case in *Dateable* that Christian young people ought to consider dating relationships to be fertile ground for practicing how to be in healthy, affirming relationships to prepare for a future marriage relationship.[5] At the outset, the authors set up a dichotomy between a life that is controlled and a life that is ruined. "The desires you have deep inside you can propel you to greatness or destroy your life in a single spark. If you can't control your passion, you can't control your future."[6] They map out how to control your emotions and passions so that your dating relationships are healthy and safe, which means they don't lead to premarital sex or the possibility of hurt feelings. What is

---

2 Clinton, *Smart Girls, Smart Choices*, 27.

3 Clinton, *Smart Girls, Smart Choices*, 29 (emphasis mine).

4 Clinton, *Smart Girls, Smart Choices*, 31.

5 Justin Lookadoo and Hayley DiMarco, *Dateable: Are You? Are They?* (Grand Rapids, MI: Revell, 2003).

6 Clinton, *Smart Girls, Smart Choices*, 8.

implicit, but clear, is that premarital sex and hurt feelings, which are the results of desire, are so powerful as to possibly ruin one's life. For evangelical Christian girls, it is best to avoid any possibility of these outcomes rather than learn to trust one's emotions and desires in a developmentally appropriate way. Being taught that what a girl wants is not as important as what God wants, and that the two would always be at odds, becomes a belief that listening to oneself and one's own desires is a sin. In this line of thinking, girls are encouraged to remain silent, to not let anyone know what they're really thinking, to reject listening to their own voices and desires, and to think that being quiet is more virtuous and more godly than speaking their minds.

Made by God This Way

In *His Princess: Girl Talk with God*, Sheri Rose Shepherd, a former beauty queen, is candid about her life as a young woman. She had eating disorders, engaged in drug use, and had a sexual past that included having had an abortion. It is commendable that Shepherd is so honest about topics that are normally off-limits for women in church. Her testimony serves as the foundation for her advice to girls so they do not have the experiences she has had.

This advice includes topics such as what kinds of clothes to wear, with the underlying imperative that the most desirable guys in school only respected girls who dressed conservatively rather than sexy. Shepherd reports such a conversation with a young man: "She is a class act. She's the kind of girl you want to be the mother of your children. The other girls are only good for one thing.' 'What's that?' I asked. 'Sex,' he answered. 'That's why they dress like prostitutes.'"[7] The encouragement to dress modestly revolves around being seen as a potential wife rather than just for sex. The author does not call the young man in this scenario into question at all for his sexist and objectifying gaze at the girls in his school. The young man is still respected as a guy who honors girls who dress conservatively, even when he says that some girls are "only good for one thing."

---

7 Sheri Rose Shepherd, *His Princess: Girl Talk with God* (Grand Rapids, MI: Revell, 2010), 55.

Lookadoo and DiMarco also fail to correct young men when their desires are sexist and demeaning. They write of a young man's intentions:

> He will tell you what you want to hear, not the truth. . . . All this doesn't mean guys are jerks and girls are great. It just means that we all have different ways of looking at things. *The balance of the universe depends on this.* Girls are home-builders—you create, you give birth, you nurture and protect your families. So, you tend to be on the lookout for the perfect home, the perfect provider, the perfect husband. *It's the way you're wired.* Guys are hunters—they have to go off and conquer and save the world. *It's the way they were designed.* So, it isn't being horrible jerks that makes them this way; it's a well-designed plan.[8]

According to this way of thinking, God designed it so that men want to conquer and will lie to get what they want, and women are responsible for reining these men in. These books are perpetuating a very dangerous stereotype, as it can make young women feel that they must be quiet, domestic nurturers to be good Christian girls and that young men must set out to be conquerors or see themselves as saviors to be godly. These gendered stereotypes are branded as *the way God intended it.* This pressure to be good girls who constrain their emotions to earn the love of a godly man has negative consequences for their ability to live robust, abundant lives as their true selves and as Christian women. Just as not all men are designed to want to save the world, not all women are constantly on the lookout for the perfect husband and home. It also contributes to the pervasive belief that rationality is good and emotionality is bad. On shows like *The Bachelor,* women are depicted as being crazy because they emotionally "fall in love" with the bachelor after just a couple of episodes, while the bachelor is depicted as rational, as he methodically determines which girl will be the best choice for him. These depictions reify the stereotypes of women as emotional hysterics who are obsessed with marriage and men as rational beings who are capable of picking a suitable partner when the time is right. As we have seen in Christian girlhood books, these same stereotypes are branded as being *the way God intended it.*

---

8 Lookadoo and DiMarco, *Dateable,* 19–21 (emphasis mine).

Confronting Lies from Satan

Nancy DeMoss Wolgemuth, founder of the True Woman movement,[9] and Dannah Gresh, who speaks about Christian womanhood and relationships,[10] see contemporary mistaken or false beliefs about one's self-worth as lies that need to be countered with the truth of the Bible. For DeMoss and Gresh, these "lies" do not come from mental illness, natural insecurities, or marketing, they come from Satan. Satan's lies inform the culture, prey on our insecurities, and can be combated only by prayer and memorizing Scriptures that speak to these lies. Their list of lies includes, "If I just had friends, I wouldn't be so lonely," and "What I do now doesn't affect the future."[11]

Using Bible references to Satan being the father of lies, DeMoss and Gresh set up their understanding of Satan's lies as evil and the corresponding truths as good. While some of these lies are messages that young women need to interrogate, blaming Satan can cause a young woman to believe that something like loneliness is a problem that can be solved by praying and reading the Bible more rather than encouraging deeper reflection on what loneliness really is and why one can feel lonely. More importantly, it sets up loneliness as a bad behavior or the result of bad choices, rather than a fact of life and appropriate response to loss for most people at certain times in their lives. It is certainly not a sin to be lonely, but the way it is framed as a lie from Satan implies that God insists otherwise.

Lies vs. Truth is one of the major subthemes that has appeared in these works within the context of making good choices. *Perfectly Unique*, by Annie F. Downs, employs the strategy of dismantling lies as she promotes a unique type of body acceptance for young women.[12] Her book is a head-to-toe look at the human girl's body, including her

9 Nancy DeMoss Wolgemuth, "Meet Nancy," Revive Our Hearts, accessed June 27, 2024, https://www.reviveourhearts.com/about/nancy-demoss-wolgemuth/. The True Woman movement seeks to return to an understanding of "biblical womanhood" that is complementarian and patriarchal in nature.

10 Dannah Gresh, "Meet Dannah," Pure Freedom Ministries, accessed June 27, 2024, https://dannahgresh.com/meet-dannah/.

11 Nancy DeMoss Wolgemuth and Dannah Gresh, *Lies Young Women Believe and the Truth That Sets Them Free* (Chicago: Moody Publishers, 2008), table of contents.

12 Annie F. Downs, *Perfectly Unique: Praising God from Head to Toe* (Grand Rapids, MI: Zondervan, 2012).

mind, mouth, heart, and hands. In dealing with the mind, Downs recommends, like DeMoss and Gresh, that young women stop believing lies about themselves (that they are too fat, too ugly, no one likes them) and counter these lies with the truths found in the Bible.[13]

Downs's perspective on seeing the body is a welcome response to the kinds of objectification and cultural valuing of girls' bodies that is found both in the culture at large as well as the church. Seeing the body as whole and connected, that a girl's mind, heart, emotions, gifts, and abilities are as important as what she looks like, is a powerful way of showing a young woman that her body was created unique and beautiful, and not merely as an object for men's ogling. When a young woman can appreciate the way her body allows her to move and do things, it is a different kind of parsing of body parts than the extreme scrutiny that many young women engage in, wherein every body part is examined for its failings and perceived ugliness. Seeing the body as a whole entity working together is to see it as something beautiful and created by God for a purpose, and Downs's work moves the reader in that direction.

At the same time, Downs falls prey to a common problem in ministry and church settings: failing to adequately analyze our cultural and societal expectations for beauty and goodness. She offers some rather run-of-the-mill beauty tips (Wear makeup, but not a lot! Wear some earrings!), but these do not encourage girls that do not fit a certain stereotype in understanding that they too are beautiful and are not making poor choices simply because they are not following that kind of advice.

All of the books considered here are written in a very conversational, friendly tone that likely only resonates with girls who are like the authors—white, able-bodied, cisgender, and heterosexual. This type of casual, getting-coffee-together conversational writing puts the reader in a position of believing that the author has the experience and authority to provide such wisdom. It is not a two-way conversation between equals, but it mimics one. Whiteness, able-bodiedness, and presumed cisgender heterosexuality serves as an implicit curriculum within all these materials. In conservative evangelical Christian publishing, as in much of contemporary media, white authors believe they are writing for

---

13 Downs, *Perfectly Unique*, 48–51.

a wide audience, even so far as believing that their materials might be accessible outside of Christian circles and therefore be tools to evangelize. These authors are not, however, cognizant of the cultural assumptions brought to their understanding of what it means to follow Jesus that are steeped in their own whiteness. None of the authors of these books felt the need to identify their social locations, because within American Evangelicalism, being white, cisgender, heterosexual, and able-bodied is a given. Neither did these authors feel the need to qualify any of their recommendations culturally—for example, a blanket recommendation for how much makeup to wear not only may assume a particular feminine presentation of whiteness, it also assumes that to be a girl who likes to have pink hair or a girl who does not like to wear makeup is somehow less in line with God's intent for girls. These books are hyper-specific to a particular brand of white American Christian girlhood but are not labeled as such.

Narrative Colonization

The authority derived from the folksy connections made in these books functions similarly to a concept coined by Brittney Cooper, professor of women and gender studies at Rutgers University and cofounder of The Crunk Feminist Collective,[14] called narrative colonization. Cooper describes filmmaker Tyler Perry's work as an example of narrative colonization when he dresses in drag to enter women's spaces (at the kitchen table, for example), empathize, and offer sage advice that inevitably reinscribes patriarchy.[15] While Cooper's understanding of narrative colonization relates to a Black man entering Black women's spaces, the concept is helpful in describing the methods used in Christian girlhood books. The messages from these Christian women authors indeed reinscribe patriarchy to help Christian girls and women follow God more closely and live more whole and meaningful lives while deferring to boys and men, even if it is not explicitly stated.

---

14 Brittney C. Cooper, Susana M. Morris, and Robin M. Boylorn, "Crunk Feminist Perspective," accessed June 27, 2024, https://www.crunkfeministcollective.com/.
15 Brittney Cooper, "Panel Discussion on the Films of Tyler Perry" (lecture, Northwestern University, Evanston, November 28, 2012).

There is a sense that the adult authors are putting on the veneer of girlhood to enter the girls' space, relate as a perceived peer, and offer advice that helps to solve their problems. In the case of *Dateable*, the book is even made to look like a notebook that has been doodled in. The perceived authority of the author's voice serves to encourage a lack of trust in girls' own emotions and desires and a repression of their own voice. In this way, as girls read these texts, they begin to conform to externally provided frameworks for how to make good choices with the implicit promise that these good choices will prevent future catastrophe and ensure that their life will turn out as desired.

Reimagining Good Girls

Several contemporary writers have begun to interrogate the notion of the good girl and the suffocating decisions needed to fulfill that role. In *The Curse of the Good Girl*, Rachel Simmons reports characteristics of good girls and bad girls from the mouths of girls themselves. The young women who participated in Simmons' Girls Leadership Institute reported that good girls are quiet, perfect, well-rounded, honorable, enthusiastic, kind, intelligent, conservative, respectful, always busy, flirtatious, skinny, healthy, average, confident, and people-pleasers, and do everything right.[16] This list highlights that girls are flirtatious, yet quiet; intelligent, yet people-pleasers; and are confident, yet average. Author Peggy Orenstein also notes the pressure on school-aged girls to be skinny, pretty, high-achievers who are also nice people-pleasers.[17]

In contrast, Simmons's participants indicate that bad girls are arguing, rule breakers, foul mouthed, artistic, don't care what people think, cheaters, liars, thieves, proud, loud, selfish, speak their minds, and are the center of attention.[18] Simmons notes that the bad girls are the ones who are more authentic, think critically, and are leaders rather than followers.[19] The good girls in Simmons's research keep their emotions in

---

16 Rachel Simmons, *The Curse of the Good Girl: Raising Authentic Girls with Courage and Confidence* (New York: Penguin Press, 2009), 2.

17 Peggy Orenstein, *Cinderella Ate My Daughter: Dispatches from the Front Lines of the New Girlie-Girl Culture* (New York: Harper Collins, 2011), 17.

18 Simmons, *The Curse of the Good Girl*, 4.

19 Simmons, *The Curse of the Good Girl*, 4.

check, keep quiet, and make people happy, while the bad girls express their emotions and say what they think.

Simmons argues that the constant pressure on girls to be good and quiet people-pleasers by not expressing what they think and feel has contributed to their being disconnected from their own emotions. "Good girl pressure places girls on strict emotional diets, telling them that certain feelings are better than others. . . . Placed at odds with their most important feelings, many do not develop the skills to speak their minds when they need to, or the skin to endure the claims of someone else."[20] As these girls participate in relationships with friends, parents, and teachers, they learn that stifling their emotions will keep these important relationships intact. They also begin to diminish themselves for fear that, if they succeed, they will be perceived as thinking that they are better than their friends and, again, the relationship will suffer or terminate.[21] For good girls, being in control of your emotions will keep your relationships pure and free of drama and you will not fall into the sin of being a bad girl.

This kind of emotional restriction leads to girls being unable to simply be themselves. Simmons notes that "[we] . . . tell people how we feel in order to be recognized and uniquely understood. When a girl is not entitled to express what she feels, she is by definition unable to define herself."[22] However, Christian materials for girls like the ones discussed here encourage young women to remain mysterious and quiet to both please God and attract the attention of supposedly good young men, and to care more about what God wants than what they want. This demand stifles young women's growth in self-knowledge and silences their desires.

When I was involved in an Evangelical campus ministry in college, a fellow student had suggested that participating in evangelism efforts would help her forget her own sadness and loneliness. This kind of denial of self and lack of understanding of the complexity of inner emotional life, not to mention the possibility of something like clinical depression, is not uncommon within conservative theological circles. Praying away the pain or getting busy doing the Lord's work is often

---

20 Simmons, *The Curse of the Good Girl*, 6.
21 Simmons, *The Curse of the Good Girl*, 38.
22 Simmons, *The Curse of the Good Girl*, 17.

held up as the solution to inner turmoil, sadness, grief, anger, and other so-called bad emotions.

With the campus ministry, I read *Passion and Purity* by the famous missionary and wife of a martyr, Elisabeth Elliot. Elliot made the case that a woman should never initiate contact with men, should never tell a man how she feels until he has told her that he loves her, and that, if she has a crush on someone, she should pray about it and keep it to herself.[23] While the explicit curriculum taught me that women's desires and feelings were only acceptable in response to men's, the implicit curriculum taught me that my desires and emotions might be sin.

Simmons suggests that if one cannot express their feelings, one cannot really be allowed to feel their feelings. She writes:

> Good Girl pressure delivers a sucker punch to girls' emotional intelligence. The Good Girl who emerges is an emotional bellwether, a projection of the feelings we have designated acceptable in girls. When girls cannot identify, express, and accept a full range of their feelings, they lose critical connections to themselves and their relationships. They are trained to reveal only the parts of themselves deemed Good and to avoid what remains.[24]

When feelings might be thought to be sin, it is imperative to not only silence those feelings but privately confess and attempt to get rid of them. Only being allowed to act in approved ways and express approved emotions, and subsequently make good and right choices, ensures that good Christian girls will be blessed with what God wants for them.

Good Choices, No Guarantees

Learning to make good choices is a crucial part of growing up and maturing, and the choices that young women make will affect them as they grow older. However, as girls internalize messages from these Christian girlhood books, they might believe that if they make all the

---

23 Elisabeth Elliot, *Passion and Purity: Learning to Bring Your Love Life under Christ's Control* (Grand Rapids, MI: Revell, 2002).
24 Simmons, *The Curse of the Good Girl*, 34.

right choices and obey rules exactly, life will turn out for them as they have been taught to hope. Many Christian girlhood books miss wrestling with the message that doing everything right will not protect girls from loss, fear, pain, and heartbreak. These are universal experiences, regardless of religious faith. Without learning how to accept that life doesn't always go as planned, Christian girls can believe that they must have made a poor or wrong choice somewhere along the way, so God has chosen to punish them or withhold something good from them.

The emphasis in these materials is on right choices based on the author's interpretation of what the Bible says rather than critical engagement and deep reflection on the inevitable choices that everyone must make. The materials analyzed here ultimately tell the stories of the right choices that the authors believed would be most beneficial to the young women reading their books. They used cultural references and popular topics of concern for girls to challenge them to put their trust in God rather than secular culture, but without acknowledging that making right choices is no guarantee that everything will work out exactly as desired.

It is also highly problematic to insinuate that trusting God and the Bible is opposed to trusting oneself and being free to express oneself fully. These deeply restrictive ideas of obedience to God create a picture of a good Christian girlhood that is white, able-bodied, cisgender and heterosexual, voiceless, desireless, and dependent on male favor and leadership. It is no coincidence that books written for Christian girls and women most often focus on maintenance of relationships and keeping your voice down, while men's and boy's books focus on leadership and adventure. The mistakes made by girls at this developmental stage where they are meant to be pursuing their own independence become understood by girls as potentially severing their relationship with God. If girls make one of these so-called mistakes, they have either listened to Satan or listened to themselves rather than to God, and therefore their relationship with God is compromised. In these materials, mistake is a code word for sin. There is no robust theology of mistake-making here because the only way to learn or grow is to repent of being one kind of girl and turn into another kind that is more acceptable to God. This is an incredibly narrow vision of God and girlhood, not to mention an offensive view of both girls and boys, one that is increasingly being challenged by contemporary movements against purity culture in the church.[25] With increasing interrogation of these cultural concepts of good, pure girlhood, a more robust and loving theological anthropology of girlhood can take shape.

25 Linda Kay Klein, *Pure: Inside the Evangelical Movement That Shamed a Generation of Young Women and How I Broke Free* (New York: Atria Books, 2018). This is the seminal work challenging purity culture in the church. See also Linda Kay Klein, "Break Free Together," accessed June 27, 2024, https://lindakayklein.com/break-free-together/, where Klein collects stories and hosts experiences where victims of purity culture and religious trauma can help each other heal through storytelling.

CHAPTER FOUR

Companioning Youth through Their Mistakes

David Penn

In *Deep Survival*, author and survivalist Laurence Gonzales describes surviving in extreme conditions such as being lost in a snowy wilderness or marooned in the ocean on a lifeboat. He argues that, in some cases, people with more expertise are more apt to fail because they've developed an overconfidence in their own competence that blurs their ability to understand the raw power of natural forces. Conversely, those who survive often do so because of their connections to others, either in terms of compassion, such as helping out a fallen comrade, or connection, as in conjuring up memories of loved ones to shore up one's courage. He concludes that "there is a dark and twisty road from experience and perception to correct action."[1] The challenges facing adolescents in the twenty-first century are so enormous that, for too many adolescents, growing up itself feels like surviving in extreme conditions. For them, the road is so dark and twisty that there is, in fact, no path at all to correct action or what religious educators normally refer to as flourishing.

This need not be the case, because adolescence is socially constructed. As recently as one hundred years ago, the period we know as adolescence scarcely existed. The word *teenager* wasn't even in common

---

1 Laurence Gonzales, *Deep Survival: Who Lives, Who Dies, and Why* (New York: W. W. Norton & Company, 2004), 142–143.

use until the 1940s. Adolescence can be experienced as a time of wonder, joyful exploration, and thriving. Yet, as adolescence continues to lengthen due to, among other things, the need for more schooling and the difficulty of finding meaningful employment, an increasing average age of first marriage, and the struggle of purchasing one's first home, all of which were once reliable markers of adulthood, the road appears as dark and twisty as ever.

Psychologist Robert Kegan proposes a framework for navigating this road: "people grow best where they continuously experience an ingenious blend of support and challenge; the rest is commentary."[2] Support and challenge are key as adolescents use cultural materials to construct their lives and understand their place in the world. As one of those materials, a community of faith functions neither as a destination at the end of the dark and twisty road nor even a map for navigating it. Rather, a community of faith is more like the stars above, by which an adolescent can chart their own course.

The 2003 Pixar film *Finding Nemo*[3] explores the ways in which adults shape adolescent lives and its themes map neatly onto Kegan's framework. The film follows Marlin, a single, overprotective dad as he navigates the dangers of the open sea in search of his missing son, Nemo. Along the way he slowly begins to realize that it was his overprotectiveness, his fear of allowing Nemo even the most mundane of experiences or the opportunity to make a mistake, that prompted the mistake that led to Nemo's capture by a local fisherman. Nemo is differently abled, and Marlin attempts to justify his overprotectiveness by pointing to Nemo's under-developed fin. Yet it is neither Nemo's adolescence nor his fin in themselves that cause the film's central conflict: it is how Marlin interprets them. In this way, the film rather unambiguously links Marlin's bumbling helicopter parenting to Nemo's rebellion.

As Marlin searches for his missing son and his character arc progresses, he meets a community of sea turtles traveling across the ocean in a powerful current. Escaping the current is portrayed as a sort of

---

2 Robert Kegan, *In Over Our Heads: The Mental Demands of Modern Life* (Cambridge, MA: Harvard University Press, 1998), 42.
3 *Finding Nemo*, directed by Andrew Standon and Lee Unkrich (Burbank, CA: Pixar Animation Studios and Walt Disney Productions, 2003), DVD.

extreme sport, complete with an X-games vibe and safety instructions any base jumper would be proud to share. Crush, a leader among the sea turtles and the father of Squirt, models an entirely different parenting strategy when he invites Squirt to teach Marlin how to execute the current exit strategy. "Let us see what little Squirt can do!" he pronounces, thus naming a welcoming environment—including, crucially, other adult sea turtles—within which Squirt is welcome to try on adulthood and perhaps fail as he tests out his own skills. Squirt is here given exactly what Kegan suggests that adolescents need: support and challenge.

In what follows, I will further explore the implications of this model of a community of faith as the raw materials from which an adolescent may navigate the dark and twisty road toward adulthood. One might be tempted to assume that the most important question is this: How might an adolescent know if they are sliding off the road into the forest? Rather, communities of faith must ask: How might we make the forest a bit safer during those inevitable times that the road proves unnavigable?

Patterns of Adolescent Mistake-Making

Adolescent mistakes come in many forms, yet these mistakes follow certain identifiable patterns that are closely linked to the kinds of communities that nurture adolescents. Identifying these patterns provides clues to the important role faith communities can play in offering support and challenge to adolescents. To aid in this task, I invited 142 young adults to discuss the most meaningful mistakes they made during adolescence.[4]

---

4 For this project I surveyed 142 people between the ages of eighteen and thirty-five. I asked them questions organized into three categories. First, I asked them to share a mistake they made during adolescence, how they knew it was a mistake, and how they overcame the mistake. Second, I asked whether friends/peers, parents/family, teachers at school, coaches/other caring adults, and/or their religious community were helpful or unhelpful. Finally, I administered the Duke University Religion Index (DUREL) to measure their current devotion to religious practice. The first question was short-answer, which allowed them to define mistakes how they wished. The second question was rated on a scale from 1 to 5 (unhelpful to helpful) and also included a short-answer portion so they could elaborate if desired. The DUREL is a five-question survey also

I carefully read the open-ended survey responses and discovered that they fit neatly into five categories: responsibility; lie/cheat/steal; social; sexual/romantic; and school. For the responsibility category, which was by far the most common, I included anything that demonstrated a gap between expectation and behavior. A few examples illustrate the general tone of these responses: "I held a house party without my parents knowing. . . . It got out of hand and several home items was [sic] ruined"; "I overspent in times I should have saved my money." These responses showed a concern for the challenges of growing up and named experiences common to many adolescents. They do not necessarily represent *moral* failures, though there is certainly some overlap. Instead, these mistakes point to the difficulty of becoming responsible for self and others in a complex world that is difficult to navigate.

The lie/cheat/steal category, on the other hand, does represent moral failures. Typical responses here included: "I lied to my parents of my ware abouts [sic]. I ended up getting into a scary situation and I could have gotten really hurt"; "I was caught shoplifting. This broke the law and social norms." These mistakes are normally moral failures and often represent boundary-testing behaviors. Many of the people reported getting caught in a lie or caught stealing or cheating and claimed that the resolution or the guilt afterward taught them not to make such a mistake again.

Social mistakes mostly relate to actions that break apart or strain relationships and were the third most common type of mistake. People wrote: "I fell out with my best friend at school, and it was my fault that I upset them. I made a mistake by telling my other friends something my best friend didn't want me to say"; "A mistake I made was cutting off my friends when I got into a relationship at a young age and this meant I missed out on a lot of memories and experiences." Mistakes coded to "social" often included things like canceling plans for frivolous reasons or treating friends badly. While these mistakes can be made across the life span, many of these demonstrate a lack of forethought common to the adolescent experience.

Sexual and romantic mistakes, while less common than might be expected, were particularly poignant. Four responses mentioned

---

rated on a scale from 1 to 5. This research was considered exempt under the IRB process at Rivier University, Nashua, NH.

teenage pregnancies, two of which ended in abortions. Others ranged from somewhat benign—"I got intimate with a girl who was seeing a friend of mine. Although it wasn't serious and we mended fences, I did not take anyone's feelings into consideration except my own"—to dangerous behaviors—"When I was 17 I got into a relationship with a 'bad boy,' I went through a rebellious phase where I took drugs. . . . I overcame it by breaking up with the guy." The responses were almost equally divided between mistreating a romantic partner and being mistreated by a romantic partner. In the latter category the mistake was typically described as a breakdown of discernment, as in, "I should have known better" than to get involved with that person.

Finally, mistakes coded to "school," while overlapping with some of the other categories, are specific to mistakes directly related to performance in school. Examples include: "I made a mistake by failing final-year exams. This was a mistake as I had not taken school seriously enough"; "I was skipping school due to not being understood." These tended to approximate both moral and responsibility categories, as skipping school is a shirking of responsibility *and* it is sometimes interpreted as a moral failing because it involves lying to one's parents.

Many of the explanations highlight the interdependence of moral failings and interpersonal consequences. Indeed, it is often not until someone felt the consequences of their actions that they understood the reasons why a certain action was normatively prohibited. Many commenters echoed this author, who wrote, "It was a mistake because it hurt my friend's feelings." The mistake was not breaking the norm per se, which in this case was to cancel plans at the last minute, but the mistake was behaving in a way that hurt oneself or another person. Allowing individuals to describe their mistakes in detail emphasized the experiential, particular nature of mistake-making in adolescence. That young people will make mistakes is a given. *What* those mistakes are and *how* they are interpreted, both by individuals and their communities, is the focus of the rest of this chapter.

Constructing Mistakes

Mistakes, like all social constructions, do not simply exist in the world in the same way as, say, a mountain range. Rather, to call something a mistake is to participate in a communal process of interpretation. In short, any action such as having sex before marriage or living with one's parents after age twenty-five may be interpreted as a mistake in some communities and not in others. As political theorist William Connolly suggests, a vital task of any community, including a religious community, is to create conceptual frameworks that community members can use to deal with the suffering, joy, celebrations, and death that characterize the human predicament. While certain kinds of experiences may be more-or-less universal, our interpretation and understanding of them is not. Thinking critically about mistakes as social constructions can help religious leaders and educators consider how adolescents are affected by and participate in this creative endeavor.

There is a certain banality in either essentializing mistake or defaulting to "a mistake is whatever one thinks it is." Mistakes are neither universal nor meaningless. Rather, a mistake has two components: an action and an interpretation of that action. These are not discrete components. For example, a person who is being intimate with someone who is not their partner will be interpreting this action one way or another in the moment. In that sense, the action and the interpretation are linked. This linkage happens even if one's interpretation later changes or if others might consider the action differently than the actor. To put a still finer point on it, the category of mistake is mind-dependent. Mistakes are nonsensical outside of the processes by which humans both experience and interpret our actions.

I want to attend more carefully to this process. When the respondent above said, "I made a mistake by skipping school," they were ascribing a positive value to attending school. Failing to attend is only a mistake in the context of the positive value of attending. Thus, a mistake is a real thing, even though it has no essential qualities outside a person's interpretation of them.

Philosophical theologian Jason Josephson-Storm describes several features of the typical process by which people generate abstract concepts such as mistakes, which he calls social kinds.[5] Three of those features are particularly relevant to our discussion: interdependence, normativity, and historical contingency. Josephson-Storm employs

---

5 Jason Ānanda Josephson-Storm, *Metamodernism: The Future of Theory* (Chicago: The University of Chicago Press, 2021), 90–104.

a term from Indian philosophy, *Nihsvabhāva*, to explain interdependence. *Svabhāva* means "intrinsic nature," and *Nihsvabhāva* refers to the negation of "intrinsic nature."[6] If something is interdependent, it gains its properties through its interaction with other entities rather than through its own supposed intrinsic nature. For example, it is only within a culture in which moving up the corporate ladder and earning more money is viewed as a worthy goal that sacrificing one's family time to keep one's nose to the grindstone could be viewed as a virtue.

Likewise, to name a mistake is to presuppose a sense of what should be given a particular set of conditions. Part of growing up is internalizing one's own sense of right and wrong or good and bad, and sense is an apt word for this. Often, people report feeling off, or excited, or nervous when breaking the norms they've already internalized. This disease is an embodied reaction to our sense that something is happening contrary to the way the world is or should be. The interdependence of material realities, values, and goals, then, is the context within which the concept of mistake makes sense.

The second feature of social kinds that Josephson-Storm identifies follows naturally from interdependence.[7] If a person views a particular action as being a mistake, this knowledge serves (or ought to serve) as a behavioral guardrail. A mistake, whatever else it is, is something to be avoided. To use a somewhat benign example, I try to teach my children to use good grammar when they are speaking. Knowing this, if one of them slips up, saying "Me and her are going to the store," they feel the mistake and register it even as they are making the mistake. The norm of proper speaking elicits a response in them. Some of their friends who have not encountered such a norm have no sense that they are making a mistake when uttering the same phrase and can do so without feeling uneasy.

Josephson-Storm's third observation is that social kinds such as mistakes are historically and culturally contingent and mind-dependent.[8] In short, many things we take for granted could have been and could yet be otherwise. Ideas have histories and are sustained by people who

---

6 Josephson-Storm, *Metamodernism*, 95.
7 Josephson-Storm, *Metamodernism*, 96.
8 Josephson-Storm, *Metamodernism*, 96–97.

embody them by acting in particular ways. Terms with an apparently simple meaning, like mistake, conceal their own histories and the processes that render them intelligible. The content of terms like modesty, chastity, charity, and so on, changes over time, whether one accepts those as moral guides or not. Given that these terms are always under construction, Josephson-Storm astutely points out that theorists sometimes get it backwards: we inquire about the conditions of change when we should be inquiring about the conditions that lead to sedimentation and stability. Change is constant. What is more remarkable is the ability of a community to sustain its commitments, for better or worse, in a world that is always in flux.

These concepts—interdependence, normativity, and contingency—describe how adolescents internalize and embody these existential commitments and how such commitments create a framework of mistakes.

Different Communities, Different Mistakes

Nearly half of the respondents in my study on adolescent mistakes mentioned mistakes relating to dating, sex, or pregnancy. This finding correlates and resonates with the researcher and author Donna Freitas's landmark study *Sex and the Soul.* She illustrates the vast differences between communities regarding attitudes toward sexual ethics on college campuses. As such, her study helps us see how adolescents both maintain and change their existential commitments as they move into the years of early adulthood. Freitas conducted 110 interviews on a variety of college campuses, ultimately concluding that colleges can be divided into two categories: Evangelical colleges and everyone else. While there is, as is to be expected, internal variation among students at these colleges, there are nonetheless discernible patterns of interaction that demonstrate how students have internalized norms. These norms, to a large extent, determine how college students perceive mistakes.

At the Evangelical colleges, young people are expected to abstain from sex until marriage, and they are taught through popular book and lecture programs like the ones Jennifer Moe reviews in her chapter that "protecting one's purity until marriage is . . . a young adult's number one priority."[9] All students are taught that men are active in sex and courting, and women are largely passive. These theological commitments are bolstered by stringent campus rules prohibiting public displays of affection and limiting the amount of time women and men can spend in each other's dorm rooms. In most cases, any romantic practices outside the traditional male–female binary are explicitly prohibited. These cultural norms often become rigid, leading to a campus culture of secrecy and mistrust, where young people are often confused by the dissonance between their desires and their internalized notion that sex outside of heterosexual marriage is among the worst sins. Freitas summarizes, "Among evangelicals, the quest for purity is always a religious quest. . . . This is a boon for the chosen few who are able to live up to the close-to-impossible standards of this romantic ideal. But for those who fail . . . and thereby forfeit the Christian fairy tale, it is a terrible burden."[10]

Conversely, Freitas describes public, non-Christian private, and most Catholic universities as falling into the category of "spiritual," because most students describe themselves as "spiritual, but not religious," not tied to the moral strictures of any one religious tradition.[11] At these universities, the code of sexual ethics is mostly unwritten and generally learned through trial and error. Indeed, the impetus for writing the book was Freitas's own discovery of the disconnect her students felt between the way they believed they should act and what they wanted. Summarizing the experience of her students, she writes, "We're not happy with the hookup culture, they said. We feel a constant pressure to do things that make us feel unsettled. . . . We live in a community that says one thing and does another. We need to talk about this."[12] Ultimately, Freitas finds that, while the sexual expectations of Evangelical students are overdetermined, the sexual expectations of other students are underdetermined. They are left to fend for themselves and far too often they end up participating in a culture that they know is harmful and unsatisfying.

---

9 Donna Freitas, *Sex and the Soul: Juggling Sexuality, Spirituality, Romance, and Religion on America's College Campuses* (New York: Oxford University Press, 2008), 79.
10 Freitas, *Sex and the Soul*, 92.
11 Freitas, *Sex and the Soul*, 26–27.
12 Freitas, *Sex and the Soul*, xiv.

Freitas's work shows that the process of norm and meaning construction continues into college and that even older adolescents continue to need support and challenge. The two poles of overdetermination and underdetermination set the conditions of possibility for the students at these colleges. In the Evangelical case, students do not learn that these norms are historically contingent, so the norms often function as little more than social control. They are challenged to keep the norms but largely unsupported when and if they fail. In the other colleges, students miss learning that their sexual experiences and expectations can be understood interdependently with other guiding concepts, like spirituality. They are required to create their own expectations from the ground up, with little to no guidance. To increase the likelihood of spiritual formation that fosters flourishing and growth, a middle ground of formative practices must be sought, one that takes seriously the importance of developing guiding concepts while recognizing the contingency and interdependence of these concepts.

Supportive Communities of Faith

Is it possible for faith communities to inspire a truly grounding faith that supports and challenges adolescents through and beyond their high school years? To find out, I examined the relationship between one finding their religious community helpful in overcoming a mistake and their current religiosity. The first finding was that of the four categories of help, religious communities scored second to last in terms of helpfulness. Family was the most helpful, with peers a close second. Religious community was third, with coaches and other caring adults the least helpful. There are many nuances that could be drawn out with further research. These numbers do suggest, however, that religious communities do less to directly shape the ethical perceptions of adolescents than almost all other groups.

Comparing the extreme values provided a useful contrast. For example, seven people named religious communities as "more harmful than helpful," while sixteen people scored religion as "helpful" or "very helpful." This seems to suggest that, among people for whom their religious community figured into their mistake-making self-perceptions, the religious community was more likely to have a strong positive than negative effect. At the same time, a difference of sixteen to seven (helpful to harmful) is hardly conclusive evidence that religious participation is a net good in the lives of adolescents.

Adolescents who view their religious community as helpful tend to be much more religiously inclined later in life, and the data from the survey strongly indicated that this was true.[13] In plain terms this means that there is very strong evidence that adolescents whose religious communities helped them overcome mistakes are far more likely to identify with a religious community later in life than those who were either unconnected to religious communities or whose communities were harmful.[14] Faith communities, therefore, can play an important role in helping adolescents overcome mistakes.

There is a key theological difference between communities that support adolescents and those that, even if well-intentioned, tend to frighten them. The key difference is whether mistakes are understood as parasitic or inherent to human experience and development. Perhaps an analogy will be instructive. In many Christian communities, doubt is viewed as the opposite of faithfulness, as an affront to God's sovereignty, or as a lack of faith or willpower. Shifting one's perspective only slightly, however, it is possible to understand doubt as the very condition of faith. Without doubt, one would not need faith because one would have certainty. Accepting doubt as the condition of faith therefore breaks the doubt/faith binary and creates space for courageous practice.

Likewise, rather than viewing mistakes as parasitic to human development or as evidence of the sinful and irredeemable nature of

---

13 I wanted to limit the demographic to only people who were adolescents in the last twenty years so there was more commonality of generational experience. I did not want age to be a significant variable, hence the limitation of ages 18 to 35. The evidence was statistically significant at p < .05, with the "very helpful" group scoring 18.19 on the DUREL, and others scoring 8.12.

14 Responses that religious communities were "helpful/very helpful" were evenly distributed across the mistake categories with the exception of "School"—evidently religious communities did not help adolescents who were struggling in school. One caveat is that "School" was the smallest category. With only eleven responses the expected value would be one response, so the lack of that response is probably irrelevant.

humankind, religious educators and leaders can view mistakes as the very condition of human growth. The road from mistake to well-being is dark and twisty. No amount of theologizing, moralizing, or even education can fully straighten the path. Yet religious traditions are filled with stories, poetry, and wisdom that illuminate the full spectrum of human grit and resilience. How can religious educators invite adolescents into a deeper engagement with this spectrum?

This is a question of formation. Many of the young people I meet are underdetermined in their formation; they have no theological and very little moral language to bring to bear on the human predicament. Others are overdetermined; they have trite phrases, like "everything happens for a reason," that do more to curtail thinking and development than to foster them. To think in terms of formation, however, is to consider a creative process whereby the adolescent, through a combination of practice, imagination, guidance, and creativity, becomes a new person in the wake of experiencing life's challenges. Youth ministry expert and theologian Andrew Root notes that spiritual formation, like musical training, introduces limits to produce freedom: "Just as music, then, has a structure that allows for deep freedom (even jazz has a structure), so too does formation. And while the structure of music is forming, it is not reductive of reality but opens us up to the depth of reality."[15] Significantly for both jazz and moral development, those limits must be broad enough to enable creative expression and construction rather than constriction.

Theologian and mystic Dorothee Soelle's description of the three stages of suffering provides a useful example of a formational structure that opens individuals to the depth of reality. Drawing on the experiences of workers suffering in harsh work conditions, Soelle describes a process by which the experience of suffering is transformed. While Soelle is careful not to describe suffering as necessary or redemptive, she does identify a process by which it can be partially overcome: "The first step towards overcoming suffering is, then, to find a language that leads out of the uncomprehended suffering that makes one mute."[16]

---

15 Andrew Root, *Faith Formation in a Secular Age: Responding to the Church's Obsession with Youthfulness* (Grand Rapids, MI: Baker Academic, 2017), 166.
16 Dorothee Soelle, *Suffering* (Philadelphia: Fortress Press, 1984), 70.

Soelle describes three stages, beginning with powerlessness and isolation, moving through expression and acceptance, and concluding with solidarity and the development of agency. I do not want to simply equate suffering and mistake-making, but the examples above do suggest that many adolescents' experiences of struggle begin with a similar sense of isolation and powerlessness. Religious educators and communities are uniquely equipped to assist adolescents in moving from this mute, isolated, powerlessness state to change, solidarity, and agency. We can do this in at least three ways.

First, religious educators can come alongside adolescents who have made mistakes and stand in solidarity with them. Mistakes will occur. We can share these stories and explore how even—or especially—in stories of failure, God and community can still work together to create beauty and goodness. Those of us who lead churches and ministries must actively create spaces in which transparency is the norm so that adolescents do not feel either alone or ostracized in their mistakes. Those of us who work in classrooms must actively create spaces in which the great religious traditions retain enough of their human character so that adolescents can see themselves in the stories.

Second, religious educators can help adolescents learn language to make sense of their struggles. For instance, in an introductory religious studies course I teach, I ask students to name all the ways the world is broken. They name their own experiences, including absent or destructive parents, and they name wider experiences such as environmental destruction and systemic racism. Then I say, to these things Christianity gives the word *sin*. We can then look at personal and communal dimensions of sin, differentiate it from evil or suffering, and begin to speak meaningfully about how to begin repairing some of these broken areas. This roughly corresponds to Soelle's second phase of suffering, which is communal expression and lament. It is the ability of an adolescent to begin naming their feelings of regret, shame, and so on, and to begin to feel solidarity with others who have shared similar experiences.

Religious educators can help adolescents uncover the patterns of their mistakes. Such patterns tend to become entrenched because of a consistent lack of foresight. This frequently occurs within a recurring context between an expectation of responsibility and a lack of ability to meet that expectation. We need not impose an ontological/metaphysical layer onto this structure that adds shame and hopelessness to the real pain and regret adolescents feel in the aftermath of making a mistake. Rather, religious educators can create a context of support in which adolescents can be challenged to identify their own patterns of mistakes. Furthermore, we can listen to young people, allowing their witness to challenge the community to be its best. The Hebrew and Christian scriptures are brimming with stories of great leaders who made many mistakes: from David's indiscretions to the thorn in Paul's side, mistakes are an integral part of every life story. In this sense, adolescents can find solidarity both with their contemporaries and with the timeless cloud of witnesses from past ages.

Finally, religious educators have a responsibility to create institutional and cultural structures that are more just, more inclusive, and more welcoming for all adolescents. We have a responsibility to destigmatize adolescence itself and to embrace young people as full members of the community—whether that community is a church, a school, or a family. This work requires honesty in naming our own mistakes. Owning our own mistakes and modeling our interdependence on one another generates a balanced space in which adolescent experiences are neither minimized, as in an overdetermined community, nor brushed aside as insignificant, as in an underdetermined community. After all, making a mistake does not diminish the dignity, goodness, and beauty of a person. It makes them, if anything, more human.

As an elder in the Presbyterian Church (USA), I was honored to speak at my son's confirmation into full membership of the church. Our congregation is small, as most New England Protestant congregations are in the twenty-first century. As I stood in front of the congregation wondering what to say, I looked each confirmand in the eye and said: "What confirmation means to you is that each person here," and I named each person, "is now and forever with you. They are committed to helping you grow, and they will be there when . . ." At this point, I had to stop as I was overcome with emotion. Reflecting on this moment afterward, I wondered if my emotion stemmed from the concern that what I was saying is not true or if it came from the hope that my words *were* true. That perhaps by speaking these words, I could bring into existence the kind of community that will nurture our adolescents, giving them the freedom of Squirt to try, fail, and grow.

Part Two

Navigating Institutional
Mistake-Making

Queerness in Light of God's Goodness in Creation

Dana Myers

Church-sanctioned heteronormativity is damaging and dangerous, even to persons of a nonreligious persuasion. It is especially devastating for queer and transgender teenagers. Through messages (both intentional and implied) of heteronormativity, especially through Christian formation in Sunday school, through worship, and in Bible studies, LGBTQIA+ youth begin to wonder if they are mistakes because of their gender identity and sexuality. It must be the mission of pastors and faith educators to proclaim a theological truth that counters the narrative of condemnation toward LGBTQIA+ young people in such a way as to reorient the predominant narrative from denunciation to affirmation. Correcting the narrative of church-sanctioned heteronormativity can and must be accomplished through queer-affirming youth ministry, creating meaningful rituals including liturgical rites and processes by which the church affirms the inherent goodness of LGBTQIA+ people, considering heteronormative policies that unintentionally damage LGBTQIA+ youth, and reimagining theological constructs of queerness and God's goodness in creation. Most effectively, countering the narrative of condemnation and violence toward LGBTQIA+ young people with one of affirmation is accomplished through sacramental storytelling. Weaving together the mystery of Divine presence in stories of how youth choose and affirm their names, how they come to claim their own queer identity, and how they eventually learn to accept their bodies as good and creative works of the Divine all shift theological work from condemnation to affirmation.

Taylor: "I Need Help."

"I know you are a pastor and can't support 'this kind of thing,'" Taylor's mom said, "but I need help and I don't know who else to ask. Sophie is calling herself Taylor and saying she's not a girl anymore. She's hurting herself[1] and now she is saying she won't go to school. I know Christians don't support gay people but I know that you love her. Please help us."

Taylor's mother was crying. Taylor,[2] who is thirteen years old, was at their grandparents' house. Their mother shared that their family had been there for about a week. Something was seriously wrong; Taylor's mother was clearly upset. Taylor had been evaluated by a professional psychiatrist on an emergency visit and had been prescribed sedatives to help with the severe anxiety that had precipitated the event. Taylor would not speak to a therapist in their few sessions except to say that they needed help, and they did not want to be Sophie anymore.

As I listened to Taylor's mom share the story of how the family found themselves in deep spiritual pain, I noticed how many times she apologized. "I know Christians don't support this 'kind of thing'. . . I know you're a pastor and you can't really help . . . I am so sorry; I don't know who else to turn to . . . I'm sorry you have to hear all of this. I'm sorry; I'm so sorry." It was as if desperation was what turned Taylor's mom toward spiritual and pastoral care, and she truly sounded as if she had no one else to turn to. Turning to the church for care would never have been an option for Taylor's mom, who did not grow up with any religious tradition or practice and was unapologetically agnostic. The only reason she reached out to me as a pastor was because I had previously been a Girl Scout leader for Sophie's troop, and she knew I was

---

1 According to findings reported in JAMA Pediatrics, 38 to 53 percent of lesbian, gay, and bisexual teens engage in self-harming behaviors; see Richard T. Liu, "Temporal Trends in the Prevalence of Nonsuicidal Self-Injury among Sexual Minority and Heterosexual Youth from 2005 through 2017," *JAMA Pediatrics* 173, no. 8 (2019): 790–791.
2 Names have been changed to protect identities.

attending seminary. As we talked, it became clear that Taylor's mom expected judgment and condemnation of Taylor's "lifestyle" coming from a conversation with a theologian and pastor.

Having the opportunity to walk alongside Taylor and their family through their subsequent gender transition has been a sacred journey. At our first visit following Taylor's return from their grandparents' house, Taylor continued to express thoughts about self-harm and suicide.[3] They were terrified of what was ahead for them as a transgender person and could never have imagined themselves to be a person of faith. Our conversations were deeply theological and spiritually oriented and clearly demonstrated that Taylor had made a false theological assumption about who God is and how they were created.

"God messed up when He [sic] made me," Taylor said. Taylor had rarely been to church as a child; both of Taylor's parents were agnostic. Their family made infrequent visits to their parents' fundamentalist churches but neither parent insisted on religious education or faith study. All four of Taylor's grandparents were professing Christians. However, none imposed much religious practice on Taylor or their parents. Taylor's parents divorced when Taylor was a toddler and amicably shared custody. Taylor's cisgender sister was kind to Taylor, but when we spoke she said that Taylor could not call themselves a Christian as a transgender or nonbinary person. Taylor's sister was subsequently baptized into the Christian church while Taylor felt alienated, rejected, and oppressed by a religious system in which they did not have the opportunity to fully participate.

Though Taylor rarely stepped foot in a church, Taylor *knew* that God had made a mistake when creating Taylor as a transgender person. Though Taylor's parents never brought theological perspectives into conversations around Taylor's emerging sexuality, Taylor *knew* that their opinion would be similar: that God somehow made a mistake when creating Taylor's body. As a faith leader frequently involved in the lives of LGBTQIA+ persons, I have found that many young people

---

3 While pastoral care can support youth like Taylor and their family, Taylor was referred to a gender-affirming mental healthcare provider to properly care for Taylor's mental health. Both mental and pastoral care helped Taylor discover means other than self-harm to process their emotions.

make a similar false theological assumption when they begin to confront their emerging sexuality.

Alex: "I Can't Be a Christian. I'm Gay."

"I can't be a Christian. I'm gay." Alex spoke with confidence. This statement did not seem to be a personal conviction established through years of research, theological exploration, or deep, personal introspection. It was spoken with the same confidence one would have in speaking their own name as an introduction to a stranger. "Hi, I'm Alex. I can't be a Christian. I'm gay." I found it remarkable that the exclusion of what Alex, who was fifteen years old, felt they could *not* be preceded by their statement of what they identified themselves to be. First, they said their name was Alex. Their chosen name was the most prominent aspect of their personhood. Second, they could not be a Christian. Their sexuality was third in the series of statements, and it was obvious that they believed that because of their sexuality they could not self-identify as a Christian.

Alex had been invited to a Christian youth camp by a former camper who thought Alex would benefit from our denominational teachings on the Moravian Essentials, especially God's goodness in creation. When I met Alex through a mutual camper, they were certain God could not be a part of their faith journey. Alex self-identified as an atheist, and when I asked why, Alex said, "because gay people can't be Christians. Duh." As I got to know Alex (who did not attend camp, though they were invited, saying they felt unwelcome to do so), their story sounded all too familiar in the lives of LGBTQIA+ teens.

Alex had been born into a household that rarely practiced organized religious traditions or worship. Alex was baptized in a mainline Protestant faith community, but Alex's parents rarely attended regular religious services. Alex's parents did not value faith formation or Christian education; although they were not hostile toward those with an active faith, they were self-proclaimed "backslidden Christians." Alex had several older siblings who were more invested in the life of church and faith than Alex's parents had been. Perhaps it was from these siblings that Alex decided that they could not be a gay Christian. Perhaps mainstream media had influenced Alex's theological understanding of what it means to be a person of faith. Perhaps other LGBTQIA+ young people had experienced victimization at the hands of non-affirming Christian parents. Alex still felt uncomfortable coming out to their parents as a genderfluid person. After camp, Alex came to small group meetings with questions about how to come out to their parents in a way that would keep them safe. They had no idea that there was any option for them to be gay and a Christian at the same time.

Incongruent Systems

Both the absence of LGBTQIA+ perspectives in religious education programs and the heteronormative curricula and teaching methods used in churches often lead to an assumption among so-called Generation Z youth (those born between 1996 and 2010), especially those who have little to no prior involvement in faith communities, that all churches espouse an anti-LGBTQIA+ theology. The demonization of queerness in many churches and the subsequent exclusion of LGBTQIA+ youth is not always a matter of telling a gay teen that God hates them. Rather, implicit societal messages of heteronormativity can be equally destructive to a queer teenager's faith journey. Many teens assume that they will be rejected because of who they are long before they even begin to come out of the closet to themselves or their community. They feel that God made a mistake in the creation of their bodies, that God somehow messed up in making them queer, or that they are a so-called freak of nature. This theological assumption can lead to damaging isolation and self-harm.

There is still plenty of damaging theology to be found among mainline Protestant churches, even among those communities that claim to be fully affirming and responsive to the needs of the young, queer community. Youth groups, in particular, can be cesspools of antigay and shame-based rhetoric, frequently from young pastors and inexperienced staff people. Under their care, antigay rhetoric can sound like pastoral care, especially when a young minister admonishes the teens under their care to beware of hypersexualization at a young age. Sleeping spaces at lock-ins are strictly divided between binary genders, leaving no room for those who do not self-identify in binary terms. Object lessons are made of heteronormative relationships, and, in many cases, harmful abstinence-only sex education still eclipses healthy preventative sexual education,[4] especially (but by no means only) in church settings.

The queer teen learning these teachings has little chance of coming to a healthy, self-affirming faith identity all on their own. This is why Alex believes they cannot be Christian. It is why Taylor is not getting the life-saving mental healthcare they need. These youth do not have— or do not see that they can have—pastoral accompaniment to orient them toward a healthy theological understanding of themselves.

Even those LGBTQIA+ teens who receive some form of religious education or faith formation often assume God made a mistake when they were created queer or that their queerness is a mark of a defect. Some have been taught that queerness is the price of sin and human depravity or that, while it is not their fault, it is their burden to bear. Heteronormative stereotypes abound in many churched and other ecclesial settings, as well as in everyday community life, in many parts of the United States. Binaries, especially the use of patriarchal and masculine-normative binaries for God, show up in Sunday school curricula from the onset of formal education and sometimes even before. For example, the animals on Noah's ark are described as coming in male/female pairs; this becomes the scriptural basis for promoting heteronormative relationships for animals and, by extension, for humankind. Many Christian picture books designed for preschool-aged children display female giraffes with pink bows and male rhinoceros with blue bow ties attached to their horns marching up the ramp to Noah's ark. In addition, many churches that rely on heteronormative theologies tend to define God in masculine terms—"Judge," "Father," and "King"—while feminine imagery for God is often neglected or ignored.[5] David and Jonathan's erotic love story is retold through the lens of chaste male friendship; even Jesus's masculinity is celebrated as

---

4 John S. Santelli et al., "Abstinence-Only-Until-Marriage Policies and Programs: An Updated Position Paper of the Society for Adolescent Health and Medicine," *Journal of Adolescent Health* 61, no. 3 (September 2017): 400–403. See also the chapter "Mistake and Sin in Adolescent Sexuality" by Emily S. Kahm in this volume for a critique of abstinence-only sexuality education programs.

5 For a helpful review of this, see Ada Maria Isasi-Diaz, *Mujerista Theology: A Theology for the Twenty-First Century* (Maryknoll, NY: Orbis Books, 1996).

a representative characteristic of the embodiment of a masculine God in the incarnation.[6]

Because Christian educators are often older adults in heteronormative relationships, LGBTQIA+ adolescents might be accepted by this generation of teachers, but they often are not understood by them. While many LGBTQIA+ teens affirm that these earliest experiences in faith settings profoundly impacted their sense of self as an older child, they fail to recognize the absence of godly queer iconography and representative images in their formative years. As I listen to LGBTQIA+ youth who grew up in mainline Protestant faith traditions, some fondly remember a single gay church member from their youth who was particularly attentive and interested in them, yet their churches would quickly usher away these strong gay influences. This appeared to be because of a fear of the sexualization too often associated with queerness or because the church has memories of ages-past sexual abuse scandals.

Alex remembered such a person from their distant and infrequent churchgoing past when visiting the family congregation with their older, married siblings. Dave always had an individually wrapped piece of candy in his suit jacket pocket for each child at church, but Alex wondered why he never taught Sunday school and always sat alone in the sanctuary during service. Dave was welcome to attend church, but the community seemed to think that his gifts would be best used somewhere besides working with children and youth ministries. Alex never met a nonheteronormative Sunday school teacher, pastor, or faith leader. The gay people they met in church were relegated to inconsequential positions of leadership, were often single, and were rarely seen with their significant other. Certainly, Alex never witnessed any form of physical affection between same-sex couples in church; they never saw Dave putting his arm across his husband Barry's shoulder. Dave was usually dressed immaculately and in a decidedly masculine style, even though, as Alex remembers him, he was clearly presenting as more feminine in his behavior and attitude.

---

6 See, for example, James E. Harding, *The Love of David and Jonathan: Ideology, Text, Reception* (New York: Routledge, 2013); Neil H. Williams, *The Maleness of Jesus: Is It Good News for Women?* (Eugene, OR: Cascade Books, 2011).

Like Dave, LGBTQIA+ people who do not fit the heteronormative mold are often tolerated but rarely fully welcomed or included in church leadership, and are rarely found in teaching positions in Sunday school or Bible study. Even though these were just a couple of congregational interactions in their very early childhood, these experiences formed Alex's assumptions that gay Christians couldn't be *true* Christians, that Alex's body was created inferior to cisgender bodies, and that God made a mistake when God created Alex's body. Alex *knew* that God was a man, that the Bible said God hated gay people, and that the church would never accept them as a genderfluid adult, much less as a genderfluid teenager.

Taylor had similar experiences. When Taylor's mom could no longer manage the complexities of a transgender teenager at home without support, she could not stop apologizing about the family situation long enough to properly explain it. Taylor's mom *knew* that the church was a traditionally unsafe and unwelcoming environment for a young person like Taylor, but in desperation she contacted me to see if I had any advice for Taylor. As we talked, it became clear that the best care I could give Taylor was to help Taylor's mom begin to see the possibility for a life of faith that supported Taylor's transition. Without a support system in place, Taylor's mom assumed that she faced insurmountable obstacles as the parent of a queer person. Taylor, in turn, sensed their mom's underlying fear and resentment, and turned further inward, becoming more withdrawn in matters of faith, sure that God could not be a part of the life of a transgender teenager.

Being God's Poem

Despite these very real experiences of being failed by their church communities, Christians do have scriptural resources to affirm the experiences of LGBTQIA+ teens and to push their theological imaginations toward a more affirming stance. For example, Paul's letter to the Ephesians can assure Alex and Taylor that they "are God's workmanship, created in Christ Jesus for good works, which God prepared beforehand, that [they] should walk in them" (Eph 2:10, ESV). The author uses a Greek word *poiema*, a noun meaning "workmanship" that comes from a verb meaning to create, or to fashion.[7] God fashions humanity, but the image goes deeper than the potter merely shaping the clay or the artist painting a picture. The noun can mean a "poem," describing God as a word-artist who strings together creative expressions of humanity in an abundance of nouns, adjectives, verbs, and adverbs. The workmanship of God, according to Ephesians, lends itself to changing and shifting with each line of prose. We are not created to be static creatures, a painting to hang on the wall or a beautiful sculpture to sit in God's gallery. We are all created to be poetry, line after line of artistic vision created by God to elicit an emotional response in humanity, to do good works of faith, love and hope, and to incarnate good into the world.

This is the theological grounding that neither Alex nor Taylor received in their formative years. It is the theology that is missing from even the most affirming congregations which intentionally or unintentionally heteronormalize Sunday school lessons and worship practices. To be God's *poem* of workmanship, a creation that is knit together for the purpose of beauty: this is the basis for LGBTQIA+ pride. Humanity as God's poetry strikes the Christian differently than some of the other, more well-known, theological teachings often associated with God's creation: that humanity is made from dirt, the earth's "Adamah" or dust-man, created to till and keep the earth and inevitably to fall from the goodness of creation. Not only did God create humanity—including queer humanity—and call all of us "good," God created queer bodies to be beautiful, fanciful, winsome, delightful, lovely poetry. "You are not a mistake," God says to Alex and Taylor, "you are divine poetry, created with the very spark of God within your DNA, God's very own image written on your fingerprints, the sound of a divine heartbeat coming from your chest." This theological grounding is something to be proud of. Humanity as poetry is theology to celebrate.

Yet the dominant narrative in Christian communities is that God's creation is redeemed. This theological commitment, while wonderfully

---

7 See "Poiema," Bible Hub, accessed June 28, 2024, https://biblehub.com/greek/4161. htm; "Poiema: Greek Word Study," Preceptaustin: Exalting the Name of the Lord by Focusing on the Word of the Lord," September 2012, https://preceptaustin.wordpress. com/2012/09/24/poiema-greek-word-study/.

encouraging in some ways, also has the potential to reinforce the idea that transgender bodies are in even greater need of redemption. While cisgender bodies are said to be marred by original sin, transgender and intersex bodies are said to be marred by their very existence. This is the assumption Taylor makes when they claim their body was created in error, or damaged by evil in some way. So, Taylor ends up thinking, "If God created my body to be a mistake, self-harm is a reasonable practice as I try to repair my body to a cisgendered standard." For many who grow up in a fundamentalist context, Evangelicalism's emphasis on biblical inerrancy, atonement theology, and original sin has harmed transgender and intersex children and teens by reinforcing the idea that their beautiful, poetic bodies were somehow created in error. In contrast, theologies that are grounded in the idea that bodies, all bodies, are beautiful and poetic expressions of the divine presence can help queer youth see the value inherent in their creation, just as they are.

Neither gender nor sexuality are errors in God's good creation. Musical artist Catie Turner explores the faulty and damaging theological assumption that God created a mistake in creating a transgender body identities with the song, "God Must Hate Me." A teenage friend shared this song with me one day and asked that I really listen to the lyrics to better understand how they felt in their body. The words are both haunting and all-too-commonly understood by transgender teens:

> *Do you ever see someone and think "Wow, God must hate me"*
> *I'll let 'em take accountability*
> *For everything that's wrong with me*
> *Can't hold myself responsible*
> *So I blame the metaphysical*
> *If Jesus died for all our sins*
> *He left one behind, the body I'm in*
> *Same hands that made the moon and the stars*
> *Got carpal tunnel and forgot some parts*
> *I don't know what I believe*
> *But it's easier to think*
> *He made a mistake with me.*[8]

---

8 Catie Turner, vocalist, "God Must Hate Me," from the EP *Heartbroken and Milking It*, produced by Jonny Shorr, 2021.

Turner admits, "I don't know what I believe . . .," and I wonder how pastors, educators, parents, godparents, and Christian communities can help Turner and others of her generation find something to believe that is grounded in sound theology and biblical compassion. It is the assumed position of many churches—even fully inclusive ones—and the default status of many youth leaders that God operates most commonly in binaries; thus, gender and sexuality must be binary as well. Christian communities must do better to respond to artists like Turner who find it all too easy to believe that their beautifully created bodies are "mistakes."

One important response to this idea is that of LGBTQIA+ Pride and annual celebrations of pride. Honoring the dignity and self-worth of LGBTQIA+ youth teaches teens about God's love for them and explicitly serves as a faith-formation lesson. Attending local pride festivals with teens and observing the beauty found all around those music-filled streets, pointing out where church services and gay pride celebrations overlap, and honoring the rituals that make up so much of religious experience all help orient teens toward a healthier theological perspective. In particular, at many gay pride celebrations, everyone can be themselves, the beautiful, different, divergent, beloved children of God that they know themselves to be. This is a spiritual practice; while affirming God's goodness in creation, we teach our teens that, if they will trust us enough to let us into their lives, we will look around and marvel at the wondrous person that God has created and prayerfully seek to be an observer and nurturer in the continued process of God's ordering of the Beloved Creation that they will one day become.

Perspectives on God's Goodness in Creation

How can we orient our theological perspective toward a more healthful and positive place? In spite of—or perhaps in opposition to—a negative theology that makes beloved children of God, like Taylor and Alex, question their own belovedness, we must ask ourselves how Christian pastors, educators, parents, and communities can embrace a more queer-affirming theology of God. How can we affirm that God creates transgender bodies and calls them good? And how can we affirm that we are all children of a magnificently creative God? Here are some perspectives that can ground a more capacious theology of God for LGBTQIA+ youth.

God Created Creation to Change

First, God created creation to change. Much of that change involves growth and development. Creative change is part of God's good process for creation. Humanity is no different from the rest of creation when considered in light of God's design for creative change within the world.

According to the creation narrative in Genesis 1, on the first day of creation, God created light and separated it from darkness. Yet these categories were not binary examples of the only ways God intended for the world to be: light *or* dark. God created beautiful sunrises and sunsets to carve change and color into the skies. Just when it is the perfect time, light gives way to darkness. At the exact moment when the world is ready for change, darkness shies away from the new light of dawn. Light grows and fades and the days oscillate between lightness and darkness. This is the sense of movement, development, and change that a healthy theology can inspire within transgender youth. From the very first verse of the Bible, God instituted change, building it into the very structure of our universe. God's creative change is unique to each day and night in which it unfolds. God's beloved children similarly unfold in every shade of the sunrise and sunset of each day, changing with beauty and precision that has been masterfully designed by a loving and artistic Creator. Why would we assume God's creative change limits itself to the natural world around us and does not include human souls and bodies? Gender fluidity, like sunrise and sunset, give beautiful variance to an otherwise dull and colorless world.

One of the most rewarding aspects of working with LGBTQIA+ youth is seeing their faces light up the first time they look at themselves in a mirror and truly see themselves for the beloved creations that God intended them to be. This might be the first time a young transgender woman tries on a dress or wears a skirt to church. It could be the first time she hears her name used by her pastor or has a friend who asks her which pronouns she prefers. Affirming change in gender identity is like affirming the beauty of a glorious sunrise or basking in the warmth of a summer sunset as lightning bugs begin to fill the dusky sky. Not only is it rewarding for the observer, but it is life-giving for the beloved child of God who sees herself in the colors painted across the changing night's sky.

God not only created change throughout the natural world but also within humanity as well. Acorns grow into trees. Children grow into adults. Our infant bodies change and shift into "new" bodies, complete with an entirely different set of teeth, longer limbs, new freckles and other skin markings, and often even different hair color. Young people grow into their true gender.[9] These changes reflect the unique creativity of a God who created human bodies with the ability to change. Because of this, we have theological warrant for helping transgender youth understand the changes within their bodies as both healthy and normal, not to mention ordained by God. Surely no adult would demand that a teen dye their hair blond if it happens to grow darker as they age; similarly, no supportive pastor should ever demand that a teen deny their gender identity. Support through change is the appropriate pastoral response to the shifts happening in the bodies of young people. To support change and affirm that God ordained such change as normal and healthy is to affirm God's goodness in all of creation, including in the growth process that is "built in" to the mechanism of humanity.

Czech theologian and educator John Amos Comenius (1592–1670) lived during one of the most contentious times of Christian history, a period of extreme persecution of his church tradition. Yet Comenius recognized the full potential that comes from acknowledging God-instituted change. Seeking global peace and a universal awakening, Comenius believed that all education was religious education and that true teachers of God's creation worked *with* the potential within each human life, not against it. Human beauty unfolds like a plant, he believed, and everything in nature "seeks its end willingly."[10] An acorn will always become an oak tree, for example, because to Comenius, the potential for the oak tree is fully contained inside the somewhat fragile, ever-changing acorn. Children should not have their potential denied nor their attention redirected, for they are made in the very image and

---

9　Kay Bussey and Albert Bandura, "Social Cognitive Theory of Gender Development and Differentiation," *Psychological Review* 106, no. 4 (1999): 676–713.

10　Craig D. Atwood, *The Theology of the Czech Brethren from Hus to Comenius* (University Park: Pennsylvania State University Press, 2009).

after the pattern of God and are called by God to grow into the person that God intends them to be.

God Created Humanity to Be Cared For

God also created humanity with the inherent need to care for one another. In the biblical story of the Genesis garden, humans were instructed to tend the garden and care for it, cultivating vegetation and animal life for the benefit of the earth. This kind of care is the concern we need to demonstrate to transgender youth exploring their gender identity and seeing the shifts of change within their own souls. Care is pastoral, Christ-like, and commanded by God. We are to care for each other as the community of God, and there is no limit or restriction placed upon the care that we are to give and receive as siblings in Christ. As the community of God, then, we are called to affirm gender care for our transgender siblings. It could mean providing access to holistic care for youth, including the biological, psychological, and social aspects of understanding and affirming gender. It could mean providing resources to parents and families that would otherwise be unavailable, such as helping financially with the costs of medical and psychological care. It could mean any number of other practical applications of pastoral care; far more than conveying "thoughts and prayers"; this kind of radical love exemplifies Christ's call to the Christian community to love our neighbors as ourselves.

But before we can care properly for God's beloved creation, we must learn more about the creation for which we are called to care. As a gardener checks the tags of each plant carefully chosen from the nursery to ensure that they are getting just the right amount of water, sunshine, and fertilizer, the community of Christ should come to learn all that we can about the lives and experiences of LGBTQIA+ youth, especially the kinds of care they need and how we can meet those needs or provide resources for others who can more adequately meet those needs. We are mandated to care for creation, other humans, and all of humanity. This ordered system of care for others is biblical, too, oriented first toward those who frequently experience neglect: widows, orphans, the sojourner (see Isa 1:17; Exod 22:21–22).

When a child's understanding of who they are does not match their biological and physical sex presentation, they need care and support.

Such care begins with an ethic of love and acceptance, but it can't stop there. Churchwide training on gender issues, much like that which focuses on providing accessible facilities for differently abled church goers, results in credibility and accountability in the church's efforts of reconciliation and acceptance. Awareness of gender identity and understanding of how many children and teens are affected and where they are within society is lifesaving information for families who feel that they have nowhere to turn for support and encouragement. Christian educators developing confidence in supporting and advocating on behalf of the young people under their care acknowledges God's design for a creation that requires care.

God Created Humanity to Tell Stories

Finally, storytelling is the most practical step in affirming queerness in light of God's goodness in creation. Although providing education, support, and pastoral care and reframing our theologies are all good first steps toward affirming queerness, storytelling has the potential to wrap all of these things up in a powerful experience that every beloved child of God will one day be able to receive. Storytelling is how we communicate God's love; it is the biblical narrative that we hope to communicate through effective preaching and proclamation of Christian hymnody and prayer. Storytelling is at the heart of all Christian theology.[11]

As the Christian pastors, educators, family, friends, and communities of LGBTQIA+ young people, we have a responsibility to name and proclaim the spiritual stories of change and care for all of God's good creation. When we share the story of how God walked alongside the transgender friend as they journeyed from a situation of contemplating death by suicide to a new reality of serving as a Trevor Project[12] counselor, we proclaim the love of Christ through our story. When we

---

11 On the role of storytelling as a pastoral practice with youth, see Dori Grinenko Baker and Joyce Ann Mercer, *Lives to Offer: Accompanying Youth on Their Vocational Quests* (Cleveland, OH: Pilgrim Press, 2007); Dori Grinenko Baker, *Girl/Friend Theology: God-Talk with Young People* (Cleveland, OH: Pilgrim Press, 2023); Anne Streaty Wimberly, *Soul Stories: African American Christian Education* (Nashville: Abingdon Press, 1994).

12 "The Trevor Project," https://www.thetrevorproject.org/explore/. The Trevor Project is the world's largest suicide prevention and mental health organization for LGBTQIA+ young people.

tell the stories of times of darkness and despair that were made more bearable by the power of God through the support of Christian community, we proclaim the love of Christ. When we talk about helping Taylor change their name on their driver's license at the DMV or about how Alex found God at the Thursday night small group meeting, or the countless stories of reformed and rebuilt relationships that these young people have and are experiencing, we proclaim the acceptance of a God who creates good things. Of course, storytelling is not a complete answer for queer oppression or the self-doubt that seems to be a common experience among LGBTQIA+ youth. While acknowledgment and affirmation of LGBTQIA+ experiences is a spiritual practice that reorients damaging theology, it cannot on its own untangle the complex issues within the Christian community brought about by years of anti-LGBTQIA+ theological and biblical interpretation.

Still, this storytelling lays the groundwork for liturgical responses that can mark a spiritual transition in the life of a LGBTQIA+ teenager. Many Christian denominations and traditions offer liturgical rites to mark when a baptized person takes or is given a new name. This liturgical practice (most often a Rite of Renaming) by its very existence affirms queerness by naming God's goodness in creating beloved transgender children in the image of God.

An Open Letter to My LGBTQIA+ Siblings

If I were to write a letter to any of the LGBTQIA+ youth I have encountered in my ministry, I would include words that I wish every minister would say to the LGBTQIA+ teens who come to them for pastoral care:

Dear Alex and Taylor,

You are not a mistake. You are God's poem—beautifully written, thoughtfully and carefully crafted, artistically drawn. Your inner beauty brings a tear to God's eye. There is no place or way in which God thinks of you as anything less than wonderfully and perfectly created in God's very own image. In this way, you carry the spark of God within your very soul!

I am so sorry the world has been so hard on you, and that part of the struggles you've experienced have been at the hands of the church and church people. We, sadly, carry the traumatic flaws of our own experiences of refusing to accept ourselves as God's own beloved creations, but that's no excuse for taking out our own lack of self-worth on you.

For every day that you would like to have someone walk this journey with you, I would love the honor of holding your hand along the way. We will learn together what it means to be God's poem, and I will pray for the day when you feel fully accepted, loved, and cherished by the God who wrote the very brushstrokes of the beautiful vision that you are upon your fingerprints, your smile, and your future. I am proud of you. God created you, and then God called you "good." You are God's masterpiece. May you one day see yourself as God sees you: as beloved.

CHAPTER SIX

Creating Communities of Belonging with LGBTQIA+ Youth

Sarah Leer

I was standing in the middle of the street, helping youth to cross safely at a large Presbyterian Church USA (PC(USA)) youth conference in the Southeastern United States. For the past few days, I had seen one youth whose gender expression I would describe as punk girl chic. They wore rock band shirts, jean skirts, and combat boots. I would greet them as they passed twice a day. Toward the end of the week, I wore my "Protect Trans Kids" shirt. As I watched them come toward me that day, their face lit up. Their shirt read "Trans Lives Matter." They stopped, hugged me, and asked if we could take a photo together. I was honored. I did not know them or how they describe their gender identity. I may never see this youth again. However, they wanted a photo with me because they knew I was a safe, welcoming adult, an LGBTQIA+ ally, and they knew this because of signals. Welcome and affirmation of LGBTQIA+ youth is a way to enact a spiritual practice of mutuality and solidarity, rooted in abundant love. My visible sign as an ally was a symbol of solidarity and love.

When we ask faith communities to extend welcome, we are asking people to assume a posture of openness. Welcome and affirmation of LGBTQIA+ youth is connected to holding a posture of mutuality and solidarity[1] and to embrace uncertainty and equity. We are asking

---

1 These phrases were inspired by a conversation with my doctoral advisor, educator, and practical theologian Christine J. Hong.

people of faith to live into abundance in the sense that we ask people to see all that the community has to offer and operate out of that sense of abundance.

Yet, living into abundance is risky and difficult. Living into abundance as a community subversively disrupts the status quo. Closed doors and status quo maintenance are rooted in fear and scarcity, and yet, they help those in power feel safe, comforted, and secure. However, the work of writers and educators like Parker Palmer remind us that our connection to fear is precisely why Jesus, who lived into abundant hope while living out the kin-dom of God on earth, tells us to "be not afraid."[2] Palmer writes:

> Fear is so fundamental to the human condition that all the great spiritual traditions originate in an effort to overcome its effect on our lives. With different words, they all proclaim the same core message "Be Not Afraid." Though the traditions vary widely in the ways they propose to take us beyond fear, all hold out the same hope: we can escape fear's paralysis and enter a state of grace where encounters with otherness will not threaten us by will enrich our work and our lives.[3]

Fear and scarcity are at the core of maintaining the status quo; radical, abundant love is at the core of courage. Maintaining the status quo is antithetical to Jesus, who lived and taught amongst the societal "others" of his day and built connections with those deemed "other." Jesus challenged the political power structures and status quo of his time; therefore, disciples of Christ are called to challenge oppressive power structures.[4] We are called to challenge the status quo, even though this is a fearful proposition for some in the church.

---

2 "Do not be afraid" appears throughout the prophets (such as in Isaiah) and the gospels, including the birth narratives of Jesus in Matthew 1:20, Luke 1:13. Examples from Jesus are Luke 5:10, in which he tells the disciples to leave their jobs to follow him, and Matthew 17:7 during the transfiguration.

3 Parker J. Palmer, *The Courage to Teach: Exploring the Inner Landscape of a Teacher's Life*, 20th anniv. ed. (San Francisco: John Wiley & Sons, 2017), 58.

4 René August, "What's Jesus Got to Do with Justice?," The Justice Conference South Africa, April 13, 2017, video of lecture, https://www.youtube.com/watch?v=_f1vXXf_eM4. As August says, that the Magi were looking for Jesus in the gospel of Matthew is "a problem. . . . You see, Caesar appoints you as King, you don't get born a king . . . king, in this gospel is not a religious title. King is a challenge to the political system of that day."

Our fear is deeply rooted in what Palmer calls the marketing model: being accountable to one's "customers."[5] Although Palmer is speaking of educational spaces, these models may also be applied to faith communities. The marketing model of institutions, according to Palmer, "must improve their product by strengthening relations with customers and becoming more accountable to them."[6] The market model inclines churches to offer elaborate buildings full of amenities or a coffeeshop in the lobby. The marketing model may also incline leaders to respond immediately to concerns of powerbrokers and large donors. The marketing model, in short, is transactional in a faith-based setting.

Churches may be practicing inclusion in these settings but not true affirmation or belonging. If, instead, faith communities live into a "community of belonging" paradigm, deeper relationships and solidarity with LGBTQIA+ people can be built. We can live into a true reality of communities of belonging (Palmer names them as "communities of truth") when we are formed and rooted in a web of relationships.[7] The connectional nature of this model moves faith communities from transactional to transformational. Following this model requires communities to stop forcing others into prescribed institutional boxes by asking them to conform to the standards of the group. Instead, leaders adapt and change based on the people who join their community and transform their spaces into communities of belonging. As Brené Brown writes, "Fitting in is about assessing a situation and becoming who you need to be in order to be accepted. Belonging, on the other hand, doesn't require us to change who we are; it requires us to *be* who we are."[8] Communities of faith can transform into communities of belonging through practices that I will outline, such as: inclusive leadership, power sharing, signaling, visibility, celebration of LGBTQIA+ people and their gifts, embodied affirmation, and accountability for past and future mistakes.

Affirmation is not a luxury, it is a necessity for the flourishing of our LGBTQIA+ youth. Lack of affirmation is harmful to youth and their mental health. The latest mental health survey from the Trevor

---

5 Palmer, *The Courage to Teach*, 95.

6 Palmer, *The Courage to Teach*, 95.

7 Palmer, *The Courage to Teach*, 97.

8 Brené Brown, *Daring Greatly: How the Courage to Be Vulnerable Transforms the Way We Live, Love, Parent, and Lead* (New York: Gotham, 2012), loc. 231, Kindle.

Project puts this in a sobering light. Sixty percent of LGBTQIA+ youth who wanted mental health care in the past year were not able to get it; 45 percent of LGBTQIA+ youth seriously considered suicide in the past year; and 91 percent of transgender and nonbinary youth said they have worried about transgender people being denied access to the bathroom due to state or local laws.[9] The Church has no time to wait, our LGBTQIA+ youth are asking us to celebrate their gifts and to enact and embody affirmation of their humanity explicitly.

Leaders Who Model Belonging

Some congregations claim to be open and affirming or welcoming and affirming. However, these phrases can function as insider or coded language. People who have been wounded by the Church are often wary of faith communities and making the risky decision to come in the doors. If congregations truly hold affirmation as a core value, then their leadership should include LGBTQIA+ people. Leadership should also include people of varying race, ethnicity, class, and age in addition to gender identity and sexuality. The voices at the table of leadership should reflect the core values of the community; if they do not, then the welcoming and affirming tagline is merely performative. Some churches may be resistant and defensive by arguing they lack LGBTQIA+ members to elevate. However, even when clergy are not aware, LGBTQIA+ people exist on a church's membership rolls. If churches truly do not encompass LGBTQIA+ members and visitors, then there is work to be done to make deeper connections within the larger community.

When we speak of welcome, we also must engage in a power analysis that interrogates colonialism. The heteronormative patriarchal paradigm that is pervasive in Christianity in the United States is deeply rooted in a history of colonialism. As theologian Willie James Jennings writes concerning Christianity, race, enslavement, and displacement of Indigenous peoples, "the gestures of welcoming, receiving, and honoring guests translated through a colonialist matrix became the subjugating gestures of oppressors and marked a deep failure of the Christian imagination to discern its real status as guest and the need to translate its

____

9 The Trevor Project, "2022 National Survey on LGBTQ Youth Mental Health," https://www.thetrevorproject.org/survey-2022/.

own life inside existing ways of living."[10] Although a lack of LGBTQIA+ welcome is not a direct parallel of the enslavement of Black and brown bodies at the hands of colonial hegemonic whiteness, Jennings's observation of the colonial nature of welcome in the church is profound. As feminist liberation theologian Marcella Althaus-Reid noted, churches failed at honoring and considering the difference among members inside the community as gifts and following the lead of those who are suffering, oppressed, or marginalized.[11] Jennings concurs by saying the church "others" anyone who doesn't fall into the existing patterns, which can often include heteronormativity.[12] In order to welcome all and create spaces of belonging that are deeply reflective of the Gospels, we must assume a posture not only of radical love[13] but also of anticolonialism in our theological foundations and in our leadership.

Power-Sharing in the Pews

We know the church will make mistakes with marginalized people. We know that part of the answer is to acknowledge and hold ourselves accountable for those mistakes. But when will we know that the shift to accountability is happening? We will know when we see reparative action, the sharing of power, and acts of justice.[14] As theologian René August advocates, we need to watch for the movement of power.[15]

---

10 Willie James Jennings, "Being Baptized: Race," in *The Blackwell Companion to Christian Ethics*, ed. Stanley Hauerwas and Samuel Wells (Oxford: Wiley Blackwell, 2011), 282.

11 Marcella Althaus-Reid, *Indecent Theology: Theological Perversions in Sex, Gender and Politics* (New York: Routledge, 2000), 27.

12 Jennings, "Being Baptized," 282–283.

13 I am borrowing this term from Patrick S. Cheng, *Radical Love: An Introduction to Queer Theology* (New York: Seabury Books, 2011).

14 Christine J. Hong, "We Are Already in New Wineskins," Christianity Unity Gathering, National Council of Churches, October 14, 2021, video of keynote address, https://www.youtube.com/watch?v=jRcr0g0_5uU&t=2356s. In this keynote, Hong discusses accountability, power-sharing, and action with minoritized and marginalized people.

15 August, "True Privilege," accessed June 28, 2024, https://www.tearfund.org.au/stories/true-privilege. August speaks about this often in her work: "So, my now go-to question as I read scripture is: what is the movement of power? From what to what, from whom to whom, as a consequence of the work, the word, the actions and presence of God?"

In fact, August makes it clear that those outside of socially constructed norms, those who do not hold power, should be the focus of the church. "Who benefits the most from the life and ministry of Jesus? People on the margins of power."[16] When the powerful—those who are oppressors or who benefit from privilege and power—are the guests of the less powerful, a subversion of power can happen, in which the marginalized people in a system lead those who hold the power. In speaking about solidarity, theologian and educator Christine Hong centers power-sharing and equity in her discussion of moving from hospitality as "centering the power of the host and assuming the space belongs to the host"[17] to solidarity with those holding less power.

> Both hospitality and solidarity spaces are invitational, but the power is reversed. So, in hospitality spaces . . . the power is really with whoever is offering that hospitality . . . one of the crucial places for people in power to understand, is that solidarity is an invitational social contract. And invitations can be revoked at any time, as a form of accountability.[18]

The practice of power-sharing is a process, and it will need to happen over and over again in order to be effective in changing the power dynamics in an institution.[19] A paradigmatic shift requires a power shift, which often means a shift in leadership structure. This leadership shift could mean those in power stepping back and centering the stories and supporting the work of LGBTQIA+ people. This allows young people and adults in faith communities to see the movement of the Holy Spirit through different people, with different voices, and different lived experiences.

When we honor the dignity and humanity that people deserve—the dignity and humanity that Jesus exemplified—we live out the liberative gospel message. The youth will respond. They will see the openness of the church; they will respond to the affirmation and the power shifts. They will see the presence of God in our actions; adults model for our youth how to be Church. Our actions are faith formation. In what

---

16 August, "True Privilege."
17 Hong, "We Are Already in New Wineskins."
18 Hong, "We Are Already in New Wineskins."
19 Hong, "We Are Already in New Wineskins."

is spoken (explicit), what is enacted (implicit), and what is silent and unspoken (null), we teach the youth what we value.[20] Youth are attuned to power structures and power dynamics and are constantly assessing who holds power in various spaces. When those with power neglect LGBTQIA+ belonging in a church culture, the institution is teaching its young people what it values, and the youth take notice.

Signals Are Essential

I once led a discussion with adults in a congregation that was centered on LGBTQIA+ affirmation and welcome by centering LGBTQIA+ stories. People kept jumping into the discussion with examples of those who were openly LGBTQIA+ in the church community. Then, a church member stopped the conversation to say, "Okay, I love what you are saying, and, yes, there are people here in this congregation who are gay, and people know them, but my grown daughter, who doesn't attend regularly, is a lesbian. How does she know to get out of her car? How do she and her partner know to walk across the parking lot and come in the doors?"

I held my breath. It was a very important question. This isn't only a question of logistics or signage; it is a question of belonging. How do people know they belong in the community? How do they know they can worship in a place that includes inclusive language? How do they know they can bring their kids to faith-formation programs? How do they know someone will visit them in the hospital when they have emergency surgery? How do they know they will not encounter heteronormative assumptions about their family? How do they know?

One way is through signals like the T-shirt I wore at the youth conference.[21] Signals are ways that communities show affirmation and welcome of LGBTQIA+ people. I once spent a week at a Christian camp

---

20 These examples of curriculum mirror Elliot Eisner's three curricula; especially important here is his coined educational term "null curriculum," meaning excluded or minimized topics in the curriculum. See William H. Schubert, "Curriculum Inquiry," in *The SAGE Handbook of Curriculum and Instruction*, ed. F. Michael Connelly (Los Angeles: SAGE Publications, 2008), 410.

21 I use the term "signals" here intentionally. In conversation with queer and LGBTQIA+ faith leaders, the term "signals" was used repeatedly and here I am following their lead.

in Texas as a spiritual advisor and kept noticing something interesting: most of the young adult counselors (generally ages 18–25) were wearing pronouns buttons. I asked several of the staff about it, and one staff member (whose pronouns are they/them) commented that a member of the leadership team had provided them for the staff. I do not know the full impact of the buttons, but I was moved to tears thinking about all of the children and youth who would spend their summer seeing such signals of affirmation and celebration on the backpacks and water bottles of their leaders at a Christian camp. These signals do not go unnoticed. It is powerful to see young adults claim their personhood and be honored as they bring their whole selves to a faith-based camp.

On the other hand, our indecision and inaction over using any signals also makes a powerful statement. Often faith communities who want to deepen their welcome and affirmation become frozen in indecision. They fear the backlash from members, offending someone who is theologically conservative, or upsetting a faithful donor. The institutional mistake here is an indecision about affirmation that opens the door for debating someone's humanity. When faith leaders succumb to fear and comfort, silence and inaction are often the result. Such inaction is chosen over explicit expressions of support. However, youth are constantly watching and drawing conclusions about what a faith community believes. This inaction teaches our youth as clearly as our explicit messages.

Moving toward Celebration

Welcome and affirmation are part of a spectrum moving ultimately toward celebration of the gifts of LGBTQIA+ people. I attended a workshop led by Alex McNeill, former executive director of More Light Presbyterians, in which he described this spectrum of inclusion; he pointed out that faith communities are in various places along a spectrum of support that can be identified along that spectrum as "tolerant, accepting, ally, advocate, or celebrate" in their work of welcome for LGBTQIA+ folks.[22]

______

22 Alex McNeill, "Shaping a Space Where LGBTQIA+ Youth Can Thrive," workshop, Shaping Our Story Conference, November 9, 2021.

The movement toward celebration in faith communities can be fraught with tension. During a video call with a group of church leaders, I posed several questions about LGBTQIA+ youth, leadership, and the stories we center in the church. One simple question was: "Who is qualified for leadership?" All of a sudden, I heard a voice shouting from behind a black square on the screen: "What do you mean?" I took a breath and responded, "It is exactly what I said, it's not a trick question." Again, the angry voice shot back, "No. You are looking for something specific with this question." Again, I replied, no, it was just a question. The conversation had come to a halt as others on the call looked around startled. The person who challenged me is a person from a social location with power—a white, cisgender, heterosexual male. When posing this question, it caused this person, with power and privilege, to have a defensive reaction, most likely rooted in fear or discomfort.

A few weeks later, an email circulated from the person who took offense at my question. In the email, they apologized to the group and said they were not opposed to the questions I was asking, they just wanted to make sure we were not celebrating one group of youth over another. This is, of course, merely an excuse. Heterosexual, cisgender, white, able-bodied youth are celebrated throughout our culture in the United States from large-scale marketing campaigns to heteronormative end-of-school-year rituals like prom.

In this moment, I realized something profound: my work *is* about celebrating the marginalized and building spaces of belonging for the LGBTQIA+ youth in our midst. Because our youth live in a country where the loudest narrative often comes from conservative, evangelical, fundamentalist Christianity, they continually hear a narrative that fuels hateful legislation against transgender and nonbinary youth.[23] As a youth worker, I am in the business of celebrating and upholding the dignity of youth in general, but when we work to celebrate and affirm the wholeness of LGBTQIA+ youth, we are working to liberate all youth.

I am not surprised by responses by people in power which are rooted in discomfort or fear. Fear motivates people to remain stagnant. However, as followers of Jesus, Christians follow someone who subversively

---

23 Elena Rivera, "'It Feels Like a Dystopia': Trans Youth in Texas Navigate an Uncertain Few Months," *KERA News*, April 19, 2022, https://www.keranews.org/news/2022-04-19/it-feels-like-a-dystopia-trans-youth-in-texas-navigate-an-uncertain-few-months.

challenged and upended the status quo. As disciples of Christ, we must always look for how power is moving in an institution or a faith community and what those in the dominant culture must do to share power with marginalized people in order to transform faith spaces into spaces of racial love and belonging for all. Underneath fear of change it's really all about power. As Hong says, "You see, what happens is that communities and people with the most power also possess the most fear of transformation, change, and loss of that power."[24] Welcome and affirmation of LGBTQIA+ people is a lesson in power analysis.

Embodied Affirmation

Christians are people of the Body and of bodies. Therefore, LGBTQIA+ belonging and affirmation has to be seen through the lens of embodiment and power. A body that lived on the margins: young, powerless, female, and poor, was the same body that brought forth God incarnate. This marginalized body was the *theotokos*: the God-bearer. The fact that she was chosen to bring Jesus into this world is a powerful embodied affirmation of someone who was seen as powerless in that context. Theologian Patrick Cheng connects queer theology and socially constructed power structures: "queer theology can be understood as a theological method that is self-consciously transgressive, especially by challenging society norms about sexuality and gender. Thus, queer theology refers to a way of doing theology that, in the words of the *Magnificat*, brings down the powerful and lifts up the lowly."[25]

As Christians, we are reminded that, when we gather around the communion table, we too bring our bodies forward, to be part of Christ's body. We are asked to give of ourselves, our time, our gifts, our offerings from our whole selves. LGBTQIA+ youth who are looking for places that affirm their whole selves may be hesitant if a community has not made it clear they are not only welcome, they are celebrated. Often the church will ask its people to share our gifts with the faith community; I would argue LGBTQIA+ folks *in their very being* are embodied gifts to the faith community.

---

24 Hong, "We Are Already in New Wineskins."
25 Cheng, *Radical Love*, 9.

Queerness is powerful.[26] We say clearly to LGBTQIA+ youth: You, just as you are, you are powerful. Your gender identity and sexuality are gifts that you bring to the body of Christ as a Beloved child of God. You are Beloved, you belong. If Jesus is the model for human flourishing, then those who follow him are called to affirm the flourishing of the queer people in our midst. In order to move from tolerance to celebration, churches must assume a posture of welcome and prepare for people entering their communities.

Affirmation Is Liberation

According to key findings from the Trevor Project, "fewer than one in three transgender and nonbinary youth found their home to be gender-affirming" and LGBTQIA+ youth who belonged to affirming communities reported "significantly lower rates of attempting suicide."[27] If youth are unable to find affirming and welcoming spaces at home or at school, the church can be a space of celebration and liberation; the church can also take simple, explicitly affirming actions like offering gender-inclusive bathrooms for LGBTQIA+ youth in their midst. The church can offer a lifeline for youth who are seeking a place that will honor their whole selves and the humanity of their friends and provide a space that affirms their belovedness as children of God.

Affirmations do not have to mean a complete overhaul of one's space or institution overnight. It can be as simple as identifying yourself as an ally in a group of youth. For example, I communicate through my wardrobe choices at youth conferences. I often wear statement shirts. One says, "Love is Love is Love," quoting Lin-Manuel Miranda's Tony Awards speech,[28] illustrating love's abundant, unending nature. Others

---

26 This idea is based upon the work of two-spirit Cherokee poet, scholar, and activist Quo-Li Driskill, "Stolen from Our Bodies: First Nations Two-Spirits/Queers and the Journey to a Sovereign Erotic," in *Feminist and Queer Theology: An Intersectional and Transnational Reader*, ed. L. Ayu Saraswati and Barbara L. Shaw (New York: Oxford University Press, 2021), 445.

27 The Trevor Project, "2022 National Survey on LGBTQ Youth Mental Health," accessed June 28, 2024, https://www.thetrevorproject.org/survey-2022/.

28 New York Times Editors, "Lin-Manuel Miranda's Sonnet from the Tony Awards," *New York Times*, June 12, 2016, https://www.nytimes.com/2016/06/13/theater/lin-manuel-mirandas-sonnet-from-the-tony-awards.html.

say, "Protect Trans Kids" and "Protect Queer Kids." I also have a water bottle that I carry at youth events covered in affirming stickers. Every time I wear one of my symbolically welcoming shirts or display these stickers, I am met with comments. While some have been critical, most are positive: "I love your shirt," "Thank you for wearing that"; and one young person I didn't know stopped me to say, "I wish my youth leader had worn that shirt." My shirts are not changing harmful legislation or policy nor are they influencing state legislatures to offer gender-affirming treatment and healthcare. But at a Christian camp or conference, youth can find a point of connection with me. For example, at an event, two teenagers I did not know noticed my shirt and water bottle, struck up a conversation, and came out to me. They then started telling me about their non-affirming families and schools. I just listened. LGBTQIA+ youth immediately recognize the signals. Although the academic and advocacy work I do is focused on affirming and celebrating marginalized LGBTQIA+ people, liberation and justice work is not done in a vacuum and is not only about queer liberation. The work for liberation affects all; as Fannie Lou Hamer said in her famous speech in 1971: "No one is free until everyone is free."[29]

Bold Visibility

The youth are watching and learning. They are particularly watching what their leaders say and do. Youth are discerning where they will spend their time; they notice institutions who are hiring openly LGBTQIA+ staff and share that information with their friends. They are watching what clothing leaders choose. They are looking for signs and signals. Both LGBTQIA+ and cisgender and heterosexual youth often make comments to me about the affirming stickers on someone's water bottle, computer, or the art displayed around a faith space. Heterosexual youth often have LGBTQIA+ peers who are struggling. Teenagers are searching for belonging and identity for themselves and for

---

29 Fannie Lou Hamer, "'Nobody's Free until Everybody's Free': Speech Delivered at the Founding of the National Women's Political Caucus, Washington, DC, July 10, 1971," in *The Speeches of Fannie Lou Hamer: To Tell It Like It Is*, ed. Maegan Parker Brooks and Davis W. Houck (Jackson: University Press of Mississippi, 2011), 136.

their friends. So, these signals—stickers, shirts, statements on websites and social media, the pronouns in email signatures—all communicate to the youth who see them. They are analyzing not only what is said, but also what is *done* in a congregation or faith community.

Claiming to be open and affirming, putting it on your website, bringing LGBTQIA+ voices to the table of leadership are all helpful, important steps, but this is not a full picture of celebration, a community cannot stop there. If celebrating LGBTQIA+ people is a core value, then the youth are waiting for the church to enact belonging in their spaces.

An important facet of creating spaces and systems of belonging is visibility. When LGBTQIA+ inclusion is an articulated value, but queer voices are not invited or centered in the community, it is equivalent to theory without praxis. Marginalized people must be invited and honored to truly create LGBTQIA+ belonging. For instance, one church may claim it is welcoming to all people in its published literature and on its website, and still only provide gendered bathrooms in its facilities. Conversely, another church that claims to welcome all people has reviewed its liturgy and hymns, using inclusive language throughout its worship services. Both churches' statements of welcome can be identical, but the actual welcoming of all people must be enacted in the system in visible ways to truly communicate belonging for LGBTQIA+ folks. Scholar and activist bell hooks talks about embodiment as key to liberative pedagogy and practice. She writes: "The erasure of the body encourages us to think that we are listening to neutral, objective facts, facts that are not particular to who is sharing the information."[30] This erasure supports the dominant culture and power of heteronormative patriarchal paradigms of Christianity. hooks continues, "We must return ourselves to a state of embodiment in order to deconstruct the way power has been traditionally orchestrated in the classroom [or, in our case, faith communities], denying subjectivity to some groups and according it to others."[31] Churches that center marginalized LGBTQIA+ voices and honor their embodied, lived experience are engaging in vital,

---

30 bell hooks, *Teaching to Transgress: Education as the Practice of Freedom* (New York: Routledge, 1994), 139.
31 hooks, *Teaching to Transgress*, 139.

theological praxis which is a subversive act in the face of the dominant culture and Eurocentric theology.

Accountability for Community Mistakes

Because all humans make mistakes, it is important to recognize that faith communities will make mistakes in their journey toward enacting welcome for and with LGBTQIA+ people, especially in opening a conversation about our own accountability. How do we move from learning from our mistakes, becoming actionable in our accountability? How do faith communities embody and enact solidarity with LGBTQIA+ youth by naming these mistakes, accepting responsibility, and doing the next right thing?

First, we need to listen to the LGBTQIA+ people in our communities, following their lead. Following the lead of an LGBTQIA+ young person means practicing active listening and asking intentional, gentle questions about what they want or need. It is important to remember that youth workers should not ask the marginalized person to solve problems themselves or do all of the emotional labor. Instead, it is about asking the right questions to be respectful, loving, and ready to change our own behavior. This is a humbling experience as a leader when you miss the mark; I have certainly missed the mark, learned from, listened to teenagers, and changed my behavior as a result.

For example, I was once leading a group of fifty youth and adults as we traveled to a youth conference across the country. By the time we stopped for the evening at a local church, the youth and the leaders were all worn out. I gathered everyone around, told people where the bathrooms were, and told people when lights out would be. Then I said in a clipped, exhausted tone, "Okay, there are three rooms to sleep in. Girls, put your stuff in the room on the far right, boys, in the room on the far left. All right, now who needs to take showers, go ahead, and let's start winding down for the night!"

One of the youth, whom I knew was nonbinary, pulled me aside. I looked at their frustrated, hurt expression and immediately knew I had messed up. I had not designated a third room for nonbinary youth. They said in a kind voice: "I don't feel comfortable in either of those rooms, can you find a place for me to sleep?" I had been unintentionally using a binary gender assumption in my room assignments even with a third room available and the knowledge that this youth was nonbinary. I apologized to them; I had let my exhaustion run the show and made a mistake. I had done harm.

Even those of us who are most committed to deepening welcome for youth in faith spaces and walking in solidarity with LGBTQIA+ people will make mistakes. It is a theological and pastoral reality for clergy, youth workers, and religious educators that we must reflect upon, teach about, and work to change our behaviors in the future. However, in that moment, all I knew was that I needed to be accountable and remedy the situation. I listened to my youth and their discomfort, protected their anonymity and identity, and called everyone back together. "Hey, everyone, okay, let's try this again. We have three spaces to sleep, the two I named before, and a third for anyone who wants to sleep there." That third room ended up including adults and youth of all genders. It became the third space—the nonbinary space to include all bodies— and it only happened because one youth had the courage to speak up and hold me accountable. And, most importantly, I listened.

The work of solidarity with LGBTQIA+ people in communities of faith is relational and it involves listening as much as leading. Church workers can practice active listening with youth by asking thoughtful questions and then by building off of the information shared by the youth.[32] A helpful model to use to facilitate active, deep listening is the dialogical spiral. This constructivist model is "the construction between two or more people whereby the dialogic process of listening and speaking co-creates an area of trust between speakers—the space between."[33]

Moving Forward

For churches who have the welcoming symbols but do not know what else to do, here are some ideas for how to match words with action. It's

---

32 Valerie Kinloch and Timothy San Pedro, "The Space between Listening and Storying: Foundations for Projects in Humanization," in *Humanizing Research: Decolonizing Qualitative Inquiry with Youth and Communities,* ed. Django Paris and Maisha T. Winn (Los Angeles: SAGE, 2014), 30.

33 Kinloch and San Pedro, "The Space between Listening and Storying," 30–31.

time to sign up for a booth and a marching spot in a local Pride parade. It's time to analyze your worship materials and make sure you are including liturgy and music from LGBTQIA+ artists, clergy, or leaders. It's time to revisit your employment, and youth and children's policies to make sure they are inclusive of all. It's time to designate all-gender bathrooms. It's time to review the policies of your ministry partners, to analyze your partnerships, and to choose to partner only with other organizations who share your welcoming and affirming stance. It's time to make sure to center stories of LGBTQIA+ people by inviting them into your pulpits to preach and teach. Do not do this only during Pride month; build it into your worship calendar as a regular occurrence. Make space for LBTQIA+ people to share their stories and invite the community to hear these stories. Donate part of your mission budget and partner with organizations that celebrate LGBTQIA+ youth. Put a Pride flag on the lawn of your church during Pride month and all the time.

Youth workers have a special role in helping move these actions forward and they can use their power at the table to move a faith community forward. Look for ways to add welcoming and affirming symbols to your ministry. One easy place to start is by adding pronouns to your email signature. Add stickers to your door. Keep extra stickers in your backpack to hand out to youth during conferences, camps, retreats. Keep them in your youth space all year round and watch the youth slap them on their water bottles. Make a display of pronoun buttons. Get rid of antiquated and gendered dress codes and challenge the camps and conferences that still use them. It is time to make sure your overnight arrangements are inclusive of transgender and nonbinary youth and children. Keep copies of affirming books related to LGBTQIA+ youth and be prepared to give them away to youth, colleagues, and families.[34] Keep copies of resources like the "gender unicorn" on hand to use as an illustration with parents of LGBTQIA+ teenagers, fellow staff, and

---

34 See Leigh Finke, *Queerfully and Wonderfully Made: A Guide for LGBTQ+ Christian Teens* (Minneapolis: Beaming Books, 2020); Cody J. Sanders, *A Brief Guide to Ministry with LGBTQIA Youth* (Louisville, KY: Westminster John Knox Press, 2017); Mihee Kim-Kort, *Outside the Lines: How Embracing Queerness Will Transform Your Faith* (Minneapolis: Fortress Press, 2018).

church members.[35] Keep a list of local affirming and welcoming mental health professionals at your fingertips. Send out information and resources when families need support. Make your office a place of overt and unabashed welcome and affirmation.

I was recently listening to a sermon on Ezekiel 37, and I immediately thought of the dry bones described by the prophet as the status quo upheld by people who are too frozen by fear to say anything that overtly affirms LGBTQIA+ youth. Inaction and silence keep faith communities wandering in valleys full of dry, lifeless bones. "Dry bones don't get up on their own, somebody has to talk to them."[36] This generation of youth—particularly LGBTQIA+ youth—is speaking to the dry bones of the church, telling us to acknowledge our mistakes, to hold ourselves accountable, and to act. The responses from adults do not have to be huge commitments. The commitments and actions I listed above are ways to start small and grow; these symbols are powerful first steps toward further action that must come next.

Personal and communal actions that affirm, welcome, and celebrate the wholeness of LGBTQIA+ people can prepare the way. Churches may not be aware of the LGBTQIA+ people in their midst, but they are there, or they will be. And churches need to prepare their spaces just as we do at the sacrament of the Eucharist: we make ready, and we invite everyone to the feast. We must prepare the way and *mean it*. The church can remain dry, lifeless, silent, and stuck, or we can listen to the youth and get up, speak, act, and those dry bones will begin to move. The choice is ours.

---

35 See Trans Student Education Resources, "The Gender Unicorn," accessed June 28, 2024, http://www.transstudent.org/gender.

36 Amos Disasa, "Talk to the Bones," sermon at First Presbyterian Church of Dallas, June 5, 2022, https://tinyurl.com/2m26s4u3.

CHAPTER SEVEN

Youth Leadership for the Church

Emily A. Peck

When I was young, I participated in a church youth group and joined the United Methodist Church (UMC) through what we call "profession of faith." I was baptized. When I was in college, I became the youth director at that same church and began to wonder if I might be called to ordination in the denomination. I remember going to meet with the pastor to ask about what this might mean. One of the first questions I asked him was, how could I be an authority in the church when I disagree with their stance about homosexuality? The pastor told me that there were people who leave the denomination over it. And there were people who stay and seek to change it. He also said that it will not change unless people who are in the denomination and want to change it stay to work to make that happen. What he said helped me decide: I would answer this might-be call to ordination in a denomination I would seek to change from the inside.

Now, almost twenty years later, the denomination has finally—and only very recently—changed its polity to strike harmful language and remove its prohibition for lesbian, gay, bisexual, transgender, queer, and other persons of marginalized gender expressions and sexual identities (LGBTQIA+) people from responding to their calls to ministry.[1]

---

1 Technically the ban on ordination and officiating the weddings of same-sex couples only specifically addressed homosexuals, which overlooked or ignored the breadth of different genders and sexualities present in those connected with the denomination. The ban and harmful language connected to it was eliminated from the denomination's book of polity only in the spring of 2024. Joey Butler, "May 2 Wrap-Up:

Previous to these changes, the denomination had become even more solidified in its discriminatory policies and many churches underwent a process of disaffiliation from the denomination.[2]

Today, I am an ordained minister in the United Methodist Church and I teach at one of the denomination's seminaries. Despite my own disagreement with my denomination on its previous exclusionary and discriminatory stance, I remained in the denomination that is my chosen spiritual home, having found nowhere else that fits my theology quite as well. Perhaps I also stayed because I am committed to the hope my theology gives me that we, in the UMC and in the broader world, can always transform with the help of the Spirit into people who will love our neighbors better. I know I stayed because of my concern for the young people in the denomination, some of whom are LGBTQIA+ and deserved to have as many allies as possible in a denomination that openly questioned their worth.

The UMC's Reconciling Ministries Network (RMN)—a caucus of pastors, laypeople, small groups, churches, and annual conferences who support the full inclusion of all people in the denomination's polity and practice)—is helping faithful United Methodists connect with other faithful United Methodists who understand that the homophobic and exclusionary language in the denomination's polity had been harmful and contrary to the Wesleyan theology that distinguishes Methodism from other non-Wesleyan denominations. They call their work a "faith-based response to institutionalized homophobia braided into the fabric of The United Methodist Church."[3] Excluding anyone from the Body of Christ is not only wrong, it is sinful. It is participating in the systemic Sin of homophobia and heterosexism. It is setting up the church as the

---

Delegates Declare Homosexuality No Longer 'Incompatible,'" May 2, 2024, https://tinyurl.com/5an3zuwm.

2 The Lewis Center for Church Leadership released a report on churches who disaffiliated from the denomination, reporting that about 25% of the UMCs in the United States left the denomination, most of which are located in the southeast of the country and Texas. The Lewis Center for Church Leadership, "Disaffiliating United Methodist Churches, 2019–2023: Final Report," January 16, 2024, https://www.churchleadership.com/wp-content/uploads/2024/01/Disaffiliating-UM-Churches-report-Jan-2024.pdf.

3 Reconciling Ministries Network, "Who We Are," June 26, 2023, https://rmnetwork.org/who-we-are/. As of May 14, 2021, they report membership that "spans four continents, 1,000+ churches, and 40,000+ individuals."

gatekeeper of God's grace instead of one of the places where people can discover that grace and live in response to it.

Churches who connect with RMN in some way have youth who have had to wrestle with being part of a denomination they also disagreed with, whether they thought of homosexuality as sinning or "just" making a mistake. I found my own faith through the youth ministry of my local church and began my ministry career as a youth minster. I had wondered what youth in the UMC who long have wanted the denomination to be inclusive of those who are LGBTQIA+ thought about what the denomination was doing while it was maintaining and even strengthening its exclusionary stance.

History of Institutional Positions

The first time the denomination made a statement about homosexuality was at General Conference (GC) in 1972.[4] The GC combined the social statements of the UMC's predecessor denominations, the Methodist Church (MC) and the Evangelical United Brethren (EUB) Church, into the first Social Principles of the UMC. The predecessor EUB statement included the phrasing that marriage was between one man and one woman. The predecessor MC document made no mention of marriage or human sexuality.[5] At GC1972, delegates voted that homosexuality was "incompatible with Christian teaching."[6] That phrase remained in *The United Methodist Book of Discipline* until GC2020, which due to the COVID-19 pandemic did not meet until 2024, when they voted to remove that phrase. The *Book of Discipline* published after GC2020/24 does not include the phrase.

---

4 The UMC, founded in 1968 by the merger of the Methodist Church (MC) and the Evangelical United Brethren (EUB) Church, is the second-largest Protestant denomination in the United States. This global denomination meets quadrennially to make changes to its polity, which is done through a process the denomination calls "holy conferencing" by a representative democracy based on population of church membership in geographical areas called annual conferences. The meeting of the denomination is called the General Conference of the United Methodist Church (GC) and is the only body in the denomination that can speak for the denomination on any issue.

5 Robert W. Sledge, "The Saddest Day: Gene Leggett and the Origins of the Incompatible Clause," *Methodist History* 55, no. 3 (2017): 165.

6 In the 2016 *Book of Discipline*, this clause is found in paragraph 304.3, p. 226.

When GC2016 gathered in Portland, Oregon, there was heated debate on what the Social Principals call human sexuality and whether there would be any changes to the *Discipline*'s language. Delegates voted to ask the Council of Bishops to provide a plan to help the GC proceed. The bishops called for debate on human sexuality at GC2016 to cease, a commission to study how the denomination might proceed, and opened the possibility of calling a special GC. A special Called GC happens outside of the regular quadrennial meetings. Such a meeting of the GC is extremely rare. This plan passed by a vote of 428 to 405.[7]

The bishops then formed the Commission on the Way Forward. The Commission came up with three plans to present for a vote at the special Called GC, which took place in February 2019 in St. Louis, Missouri. The delegates to GC2019 were the same as the delegates to GC2016, meaning that updates to the representative democracy would not happen until the next quadrennium. The most conservative of the options proposed by the Commission, called the Traditional Plan, was adopted by a vote of 438 to 384.[8]

Only 7 percent of the delegates to GC2019 were young people, which, according to the UMC, is anyone up to age thirty-five. Delegates are members of the denomination who attend worship regularly, meet as a delegation regularly, pour over hundreds of pieces of legislation, and give their time (away from school if they are youth) to be a part of the legislative body of the denomination. As mainline denominations are losing members and losing young members at a particularly rapid pace,[9] these young people may be an anomaly, but they are a dedicated and faithful anomaly who take their faith seriously.

---

7 Heather Hahn and Sam Hodges, "GC2016 Puts Hold on Sexuality Debate," United Methodist News Service, May 18, 2016, https://www.umnews.org/en/news/bishops-ask-for-hold-on-sexuality-debate.

8 Kathy L. Gilbert, Heather Hahn, and Joey Butler, "2019 General Conference Passes Traditional Plan," United Methodist News Service, February 26, 2019, https://www.umnews.org/en/news/gc2019-daily-feb-26.

9 For example, "In US, Decline of Christianity Continues at Rapid Pace," Pew Research Center's Religion & Public Life Project, October 17, 2019, https://www.pewresearch.org/religion/2019/10/17/in-u-s-decline-of-christianity-continues-at-rapid-pace/; Michael Lipka, "Mainline Protestants Make up Shrinking Number of US Adults," Pew Research Center, May 18, 2015, https://www.pewresearch.org/fact-tank/2015/05/18/mainline-protestants-make-up-shrinking-number-of-u-s-adults/; Cat Wise and Kira Wakeam, "Millennials Are Leaving Organized Religion.

Some of the young people, including both delegates and observers, present at GC 2019 read a statement prior to taking the vote on the plans from the Commission. Young people asked delegates to support the One Church Plan, which would have allowed individual churches and annual conferences to practice contextually appropriate inclusion and support of LBGTQIA+ people in the church. The full statement also was circulated online so that young people who were not in St. Louis could also sign. Within thirteen hours of its circulation, it garnered 15,529 signatures from United Methodist young people. In part, what the young people at GC read said:

> We the young people of the United Methodist Church are not of one mind when it comes to inclusion of our LGBTQ siblings in Christ. And yet through working together, sharing stories, and worshipping side by side we have seen each other's gifts and fruits for ministry! We have witnessed the incredible ways that God is working through each of us in our own unique contexts. We believe that if we are truly a body we need each other. We need one another, in all of our diversity—to fulfill our call to be the Body of Christ. We as the church need to stop the harm that is done when we debate one another's humanity and worth, and focus on our shared mission to live into our primary identity as God's children.[10]

This statement shows a deep theological commitment to the unity of the Body of Christ in the presence of differences around theologies about human sexuality. Those who are committed to Christian religious education with youth must take the young people's statement from GC2019 seriously and respond to the leadership they displayed. That so many youth from outside of the meeting mobilized by those present also signed on so quickly shows that these youth are using their voices whether or not they have votes. It also shows that many, and perhaps most, young people in the denomination think that what the General Conference decided in 2019 was a mistake.

Here's Where Some Are Finding Community," PBS, January 2, 2020, https://www.pbs.org/newshour/show/millennials-are-leaving-organized-religion-heres-where-some-are-finding-community.

10 "Young People's Statement—General Conference 2019," UMC YoungPeople, February 26, 2019, https://www.umcyoungpeople.org/lead/young-peoples-statement-general-conference-2019.

Since they identify in some way with RMN, I had anticipated that the youth I spoke with would think that the church was making a mistake when they reflected on the votes of 2019. I was not sure how they would interpret that mistake or their part in it. I did not know if they would have the theological language to see what the church was doing as something aligned with Sin. When it comes to faithfully dissenting responses to the church's stance (and indecision) around human sexuality, it is the young people who can, should be, and are able to teach the wider church. This is especially true of youth raised in congregations who teach their youth to be leaders and educate them about UMC polity.

In the end, each of the churches where I interviewed youth, youth workers, and pastors has helped educate their youth in such a way that they have effectively become community organizers in their local churches and, to some extent, in the denomination as a whole. Taking seriously that the church was wrong about their polity around homosexuality and those who identify as homosexual,[11] these youth leaders were ready to be part of leading the denomination to a more just and grace-filled future.

Three Churches

The churches profiled all identify as progressive and did not agree with the GC2019 decision. Each of them have been educating their youth to be community organizers, though none of the people I spoke with used that term. Quoting the Funder's Collaborative on Youth Organizing, Gregg Moder, a professor in practical theology at Azuza Pacific University, writes, "Ultimately, youth organizing seeks to develop within a neighborhood or community a base of young people committed to altering power relationships and creating meaningful institutional change."[12] This is what is happening with the youth at these churches;

---

11 The UMC does not have any statements in the Book of Discipline about sexuality or gender more broadly expressed. There are no statements about those who identify as queer, transgender, or bisexual, for example.

12 Gregg Moder, "Bridging Youth Ministry Gaps through Youth Organizing: Actuating Urban Teens as Transformative Community Leaders," *Journal of Youth Ministry* 18, no. 1 (2020): 17.

and it is happening as an act of faith in response to the denomination's sinfulness in excluding from full participation those who are fully loved by God.[13]

Grace United Methodist Church

Michael is seventeen, believes he is straight, and is mixed Asian American. Michael's parents come from two different Asian countries, one of which is in south Asia. Leo B. is fifteen, questioning his sexuality, and first told me he is white. He then clarified that he usually says he is white because people don't believe him when he says he is part Asian because he presents as white. Peyton is seventeen, bisexual, and mixed-race white and Asian. All three youth identify with the male gender.[14] The pastor of Grace UMC, the Rev. Paul Emerick, described the congregation as being progressive, with many members who have been in the denomination for their whole lives.[15] The congregation, which is in suburban Washington, DC, is economically privileged, reflecting their surrounding community. They are a majority white congregation, with

---

13 Due to the COVID-19 pandemic, my research with youth had to pause shortly after it began, and GC2020 was delayed until spring 2024. My interviews at Grace UMC took place before the COVID-19 pandemic and included youth. My conversations with Trinity and Boston Avenue took place during the pandemic and included only adults. Those youth I was able to speak with and the adults who minister with youth during this difficult time in the denomination offer important insights into how youth think about human sexuality, their theologies of engagement with a denomination they disagree with, and the ways they live out their faith. In order to protect the youth at Grace, I use pseudonyms chosen by the people I interviewed and am not using the real name of the church. The adults I spoke with at Trinity and Boston Avenue consented to having their real names used in this chapter. The pastor I interviewed from Boston Avenue gave permission for the name of her church to also be used in this chapter. Trinity is a pseudonym. These three churches are in different places in their relationship to the Reconciling Ministries Network. Grace became a member of the network within the last several years, Trinity has been a member since 1991, and Boston Avenue is not a member, but their youth groups (along with several other small groups within the church) are. My protocol was approved by the Institutional Review Board at Garrett-Evangelical Seminary, and I am grateful for their support and insights even as I adapted to interviewing online due to the pandemic.

14 Leo B., Michael, and Peyton. Personal interview by Emily A. Peck. Suburb of Washington, DC, March 1, 2020.

15 Paul Emerick. Personal interview by Emily A. Peck. Suburb of Washington, DC, February 26, 2020.

about 25 to 30 percent of their Sunday attendance being eighteen and under.

Grace's journey to becoming a reconciling congregation began with the youth group. Moder writes that youth organizing "requires the curation of certain power sharing capacities for adult allies who seek to become helpful and effective partners."[16] According to Paul, some key adults at Grace have these capacities. They "assisted and equipped" the youth who "had been doing their own work and felt that the congregation was called to be a reconciling church." When the youth group brought the proposal to the church council about ten years ago, the community responded by beginning a discernment process.

After six years, including small groups, speakers, discernment, and a year-long pause due to pastoral change, the congregation voted 90 percent in favor of becoming a reconciling church. At the meeting where that vote took place, the youth came to remind the congregation that they had been the ones who initiated the process and encouraged it to keep going. They expressed their pride that the congregation had listened to them and they shared with the church that, based on their own context for ministry, namely their high school, this vote needed to happen so that they could help their peers know that the church was a safe place. They saw it as necessary for evangelism.

However, the youth also held the church accountable for how the process happened. Paul remembers, "and then they also said, we have seen the way that you treat each other in this process. And we are surprised at the way Christian adults treat each other sometimes and we're really disappointed." Paul worries that youth who experienced the process at the church and left for college shortly thereafter may have a "wilderness experience that maybe they wouldn't have had if people hadn't been so mean to each other."[17] It is also true that through their education and formation at Grace, which includes being taught to organize

---

16 Moder, "Bridging Youth Ministry Gaps," 18.

17 The concern over what happens to youth when they are involved in a congregation in conflict is not Paul's alone. For more insights about what this can mean for youth, their faith development, and their vocations, see Joyce Ann Mercer, "Calling amid Conflict: What Happens to the Vocations of Youth When Congregations Fight?," in *Greenhouses of Hope: Congregations Growing Young Leaders Who Will Change the World*, ed. Dori Grinenko Baker (Herndon, VA: Alban Institute, 2010), 165–190.

for institutional change, the youth were able to not only notice when the congregation was not acting as they should, but also to give voice to their disappointment in such a way that the congregation would hear it.

Youth were on the reconciling discernment team and the General Conference response team, which was a group set up to respond to denominational actions, and on the inclusion team, which has been active since 2016. The youth attend congregational meetings regularly and according to Paul are some of the most informed people in the room. He also notes that the youth who are most involved come from families who are the most involved and active in the church.[18] Paul reflects that the youth, like the rest of the church, seem to be committed to inclusion as a justice issue first and as a theological issue second. He says that faith is very important to the youth and that "reason and experience have necessarily shaped [their] theology especially when it comes to these most divisive and significant issues in the church and the world."

Leo remembers hearing about the decision of GC2019. He found out in his science class and says it was "really disheartening to hear how it went. . . . At that point I didn't know what to do because we had been really hopeful." Michael reflects as an ally to LGBTQIA+ people and agreed that "disheartening" was the right word for it. He grapples with the implication of being affiliated with a church that "didn't make the vote" but being associated with the denomination that did. He says it felt like "a betrayal of what I felt the church stood for." He is on a journey when it comes to his Christian formation, saying that he has always been confused and "a bit hazy" when it comes to "God and Scripture," but that he is not at all unclear about what he calls "the staple values of the church." For him, these are the things he learned through youth group, like "loving thy neighbor, being accepting to everyone in the community, and treating everyone besides yourself as kind of like your brother or sister." He says when the denomination voted for the

---

18 This is consistent with the research from the National Study on Youth and Religion, as explained in Kenda Creasy Dean, *Almost Christian: What the Faith of Our Teenagers Is Telling the American Church* (Oxford: Oxford University Press, 2010): "the religiosity of American teenagers must be read primarily as a reflection of their parents' religious devotion (or lack thereof) . . ." (3).

Traditional Plan, they rejected the opportunity to make the community more open and to subvert "archaic" norms that do not apply today.

Peyton recounts that of all the youth, he was following GC2019 the most closely. He was actively involved in the inclusion team, helped create informational brochures to help educate the church about what plans the denomination were considering, and helped members of the church sign up as individual members of the RMN. He says the main feeling he had in response to the GC2019 decision was anger. He says, "I was surprised and I was angry that something that I saw as such a core value of the United Methodist Church was, in my view, being ignored. And the platform that I saw that should be used for inclusion and love and such was being perverted in such a way." He also says that his first reaction was that their congregation should have left the UMC because the denominational vote went against the vote that the congregation had recently taken to become reconciling.

Peyton says even though leaving was his initial reaction, now he sees Grace's important role as a reconciling congregation within the denomination by bearing witness to inclusion and continuing to work for change. He recognized that a denominational split was a foregone conclusion and wants Grace to be a part of helping whatever emerges from a split to be as inclusive as possible. Peyton's empowerment as a leader in the congregation has helped him to imagine how he can lead in a bigger way, even to the extent of helping shape whatever comes after the current UMC splits in some way. His agency has been enhanced and nurtured by his congregation, which takes seriously the leadership youth can provide.

Boston Avenue United Methodist Church

Rev. Sara Montgomery was an associate minister at Boston Avenue UMC in Tulsa, Oklahoma, at the time of our interview.[19] She had responsibilities in missions, outreach, social justice ministries, and their modern worship service. The church is a larger one. Between its worship television ministry, which has been a part of their church for about forty years, it has about 1,500 people who worship there each Sunday. The congregation is urban, predominately white, and upper

---

19 Sara Montgomery. Personal interview by Emily A. Peck. Zoom, April 20, 2021.

middle class; approximately 10 percent of the church identifies as people of color, including Native American. Boston Avenue is a vocal and progressive church, though it does also have some more conservative members.

Like Grace, the youth at Boston Avenue are leaders in the church when it comes to choosing to be a welcoming space for Christians who identify as LGBTQIA+. Sara recalled that the senior pastor of the church said that becoming a reconciling church would be "too controversial and hard for them to be able to vote on." However, the church is known in Tulsa to be a progressive and welcoming place. In fact, the city's Gay Pride parade kicks off from the church. Additionally, in December 2019 the church voted to allow their clergy to officiate over same-sex weddings in the sanctuary of the church; both actions were prohibited by the *Book of Discipline* until GC2020/24.[20] The congregation is aware of what is happening around sexuality in the denomination. They have engaged in congregational conversations, heard sermons about it, and engaged in prayer around it. In the lead-up to GC2019, the church also held monthly "resistance worship" services.

Both youth groups at Boston Avenue responded to GC2019 by beginning the process toward becoming reconciling; two other groups in the church followed suit. The youth initiated this process by reaching out to Sara and another of the associate ministers, who had been pastor of another church when it became reconciling. After the groundwork had been laid, it took about two-and-a-half months for the youth groups to each vote to become reconciling. Sara notes that there was no pushback at the time and the youth groups encountered no roadblocks with the church or their parents in their process. Importantly, she says when two other groups, both Sunday school classes, chose to become reconciling and were crafting their reconciling belief statements, they asked to use the youth groups' statements on which to base their own.

When asked what helped the youth embrace leadership in this area, Sara points to a few things. One is that the youth work on inclusivity inside and outside of the church. For example, several youth are responsible for forming LGBTQIA+ ally groups in their high schools. One

---

20 *The Book of Discipline of the United Methodist Church, 2016* (Nashville: The United Methodist Publishing House, 2016), 278.

youth formed such a group for her peers at her Catholic high school, where they were not permitted to meet. Instead, this group meets at Boston Avenue and adults from the church provide pizza and supervision for those meetings. When some of the youth wanted to form ally groups at their high schools, they came to the church for resources.

Sara thinks the adult leadership in the youth group also helped form the youth for leadership toward explicit inclusion. For three years the senior youth group has had a youth pastor who uses they/them pronouns and identifies as LGBTQIA+. Their presence and ministry helped the youth have conversations about the importance of inclusivity in the church prior to GC2019. The youth group also has members who are LGBTQIA+ and the groups "wanted to make sure that they were creating a safe place for everyone that was a part of their youth group." These youth also felt it was important to create a safe space for anyone who was not a part of the youth group or church but might be in the future. In other words, this decision was partly about evangelism.

Youth were also motivated by negative experiences at summer camp in 2017. That summer, several youth attended an annual conference camp where they experienced policies that made it "a very unsafe space for some of our youth that were gender nonconforming or a little bit more gender fluid or just present within a way that was not what everyone else was expecting." Upon returning from camp, the youth helped rewrite policies at their church so that they would be "better for youth that are non-gender-conforming and are more gender fluid or are even transitioning." Sara sees this process was especially empowering for the youth. They were able to respond to an unsafe experience in a constructive way by making sure their church policies were safer.[21]

Perhaps the most important reason that the youth knew they could lead the congregation in becoming reconciling is that Boston Avenue intentionally cultivates leadership in youth. Like at Grace, the youth

---

21 Kate Ott and Lorien Carter advocate for "holistic sexuality education from a Christian theological perspective [which] values the goodness of creation and celebrates an incarnational Savior which intersects with the embodied experience of joy." Kate Ott and Lorien Carter, "Revisioning Sexuality: Relational Joy and Embodied Flourishing," *Journal of Youth and Theology* 20, no. 1 (2021): 61. That these youth have been educated about sexuality in such a way in their congregations is clearly part of why they are so keenly interested in responding to their denomination's exclusive polity and wanting to be part of something inclusive in their local churches.

have adults with the capacities to empower them as trusted peers who are leading the congregation. Youth are involved in worship leadership every week; they are the choir for the early worship service. Youth give the reports on youth ministry to the administrative council. Sara says that worship leadership in particular has "shaped and framed them."

Boston Avenue also has an intentional and unique leadership program for youth called Leaders in Training (LIT). Despite the program's name, it is clear that the youth are leaders in the present and not only training for leadership at some point in the future. When the youth serve with the children's ministry programing, Vacation Bible School, or in the nursery, for example, they earn LIT credit, which can be turned into money for youth mission or choir trips. Sara is careful to note that, while being leaders with children, the youth are not babysitting but are instead helping to facilitate conversations about faith. This means not only that the youth are helpful in the faith formation of those who are younger than they are, but also that the youth are empowered to make meaningful change in the congregation.

These efforts are not new parts of ministry with youth at Boston Avenue. Sara points out that some of the staff at the church grew up at Boston Avenue, and these leadership aspects were part of their experience in youth group when they were teenagers. Through this particular case study, religious educators can hear clearly how important it is to intentionally nurture youth as leaders.

Trinity United Methodist Church

At Trinity United Methodist Church in New York City, I interviewed the youth director, the associate pastor, and the senior pastor in March 2021. The youth director is Carter Baxter, who is transgender and a seminary student.[22] The associate pastor is the Rev. Lea Matthews, who identifies as queer and whose responsibilities include children and family ministries, as well as oversight of the youth director. She is also a youth parent. The pastor is the Rev. Dr. K Karpen, who has no direct responsibility over the youth and is a former youth parent.[23] Lea

---

22 Carter Baxter. Personal interview by Emily A. Peck. Zoom, March 16, 2021.
23 K Karpen and Lea Matthews. Personal interview by Emily A. Peck. Zoom, March 17, 2021.

describes Trinity as a "mid-size urban church that prides itself on being a diverse group of folks that is in the congregation and that serves the direct community around it. And it is an unabashed and proud progressive Christian hub." This church has been a reconciling congregation since 1991. K noted that the vote was unanimous, "and I chalk that up to the power of Scripture if you really spend time with Scripture and also the power of the Holy Spirit and the power of people who are just steeped in the faith in such a way that they have the ability to discern what's gospel from what's not."

The youth at Trinity have never known their church to be anything other than reconciling. Carter points out, however, that the term "reconciling" seems to have fallen by the wayside. He has never heard people use the word because "a lot of people don't feel like it goes far enough." K agrees, saying that he feels the term "reconciling" just did not work anymore after GC2019, and the congregation "parted company with it" after that. Lea recounts that when the congregation went through a process of rebranding, which included a new mission statement and new images and symbols for the church to use, they took an intentional step away from using "reconciling" and instead embraced "affirming" because the church celebrates different pieces of identity, including sexuality and "we put them specifically in our membership vows and our confirmation vows and our baptismal vows."

Trinity, including the youth, was "acutely" aware of what was happening with the UMC leading up to and including GC2019. Carter noted that in between one GC and the next, the youth are really not that aware of what is happening in the denomination, which may be an indicator of how the church has moved past "reconciling" and the "issues" of the UMC as they seek to embrace their own identity as a church invested in queer liberation. He says that the youth group now is younger, mostly in middle school, and about half of the youth are new to the church. The youth are just "generally aware that [Trinity] is an affirming and welcoming place to everybody. And I think they think it's cool that there's queer people in leadership and they are aware that that's unique sometimes in Christianity in the United States." Because GC2020/24 was rescheduled three times due to the COVID pandemic, there were no ongoing efforts to educate the youth about how the denomination works and the ongoing conflict.

Instead, the youth, and the whole church, have focused on antiracism, housing unhoused people during the pandemic, and immigration justice.

Trinity sent twenty church members to GC2019 as witnesses for inclusion. Two of those members were youth, whose way the church paid. These two youth were a part of a cohort of older youth who were very involved in the lead-up to GC2019. Lea remembers that they were "a part of that history and that justice work and Gay pride, so [going to General Conference] was a natural connection for them." According to K, the church decided to pay to send the two youth to GC2019 because they wanted to make sure youth were present, but also for two other reasons. First, the youth wanted to be there, and second because of their vocational interests. One of the youth is a videographer and the other is a photographer.

K remembers that the youth were "both interested in being there also to . . . figure out how to interpret whatever happened, especially to a younger crowd." Lea recalls one of the youth mothers saying to them, "Don't you want to witness? Don't you want to be a part of what's happening in your church, it's *your* church, too, they aren't telling you that, but it is your church." Lea says, "they did want to witness it and they did want to document it. And it became *crucial* for them to be there to document it, as it turns out, which we would have had no way of knowing. But they got into places that they really should not have been." K laughed in agreement as he remembers that these two youth somehow talked themselves into getting press credentials. They were able to tell the story of what was happening, just as they had hoped. Some of their work even made it into national news. Trinity supports youth as leaders and educates them about how to be part of community organizing for change in the denomination.

By the time of GC2019, many of the youth were aware of what was happening on a denominational level and had previously decided they would not join the church and be confirmed in the faith because of the denomination's exclusive stances against LGBTQIA+ members and clergy. Surprisingly, after GC2019 they decided they would join their church, even as the denomination had voted to become more conservative. K recounts they made this decision "because of the witness that they saw of church members putting it on the line, taking over the stage, whatever they were doing—we were doing—that witness gave them (and [two of them] were queer) and they decided yep, we're joining, we're signing up for this, whereas they had said 'no, thank you' after the class." This decision on their part helped lead the church to take more seriously what it means to be a member of the community of their church. Lea notes that now there are conversations for new members' classes and confirmation classes about what it means to be in a community and connected to an institution "knowing that institutions will *always* fail us." Church members share their stories of the complexities of belonging and how they made the decision to join the church. Lea says that now "we make it as transparent as possible so that kids don't get the wrong impression to think [they are] joining a perfect place."

One of the current youth, a twelve-year-old, wrote for the church's Lenten devotional in 2020.[24] In her devotion, she described the effect of the 2019 Judicial Council ruling, the judicial branch of the UMC, which largely upheld as constitutional the Traditional Plan that was voted into practice at GC2019.[25] The Judicial Council was asked to evaluate the Traditional Plan, including its amendments for constitutionality with the *Discipline*. She felt the impact of their ruling that the Traditional Plan is constitutional personally, as the child of two mothers (one of whom is a clergy person in the UMC). She started experiencing anxiety and needed the help of a doctor to understand what was happening. She wrote that doing meditations with her mama helps and so, too, does reminding herself that, "God isn't excluding queer people, the denomination is."

Moving Forward

The United Methodist Church has split. GC2020/24 was tasked with solidifying the process of the split. As David Crary with the Associated Press reports, a new denomination, the Global Methodist Church

---

24 This devotional booklet is available online, but to protect the identity of this youth, and due to the fact that I was not given permission to use the real name of this church, I will not include the link for it here. It was uploaded to the church's website March 1, 2020, and accessed May 11, 2021.

25 "What Did the Judicial Council Decide about the Traditional Plan?," United Methodist Communications, April 29, 2019, https://www.umc.org/en/content/ask-the-umc-what-did-the-judicial-council-decide-about-the-traditional-plan.

(GMC), was formed by some of the most conservative churches of the United Methodist Church.[26] Additionally, many churches have chosen to follow a process for disaffiliating from the denomination, a temporary process that was put in place after GC2019 for churches who disagreed with the stance of the denomination's polity around sexuality and sexual orientation. Some of these churches have joined the new GMC denomination; many have chosen to remain independent. For United Methodists, what their denomination will look like going forward from GC2020/24 is still unknown. The polity has been changed; how it will play out regionally and how the church will (or will not) undergo a process of reconciliation and repentance for the harm caused by the language being present for so long is still unclear. But those who are in ministry with UMC youth have a lot to learn from Grace, Boston Avenue, and Trinity.

Youth who have been formed and educated in inclusive congregations have already been teaching their churches, even as the churches also teach them. Taught to organize as a part of their faith, the youth at Grace led their congregation in becoming reconciling and held the adults accountable for their behavior leading up to the vote to become reconciling. The youth at Boston Avenue began exploring sexuality and the conflict in the denomination with their youth pastor at the time, but it is the youth who taught their church that affiliating with RMN matters as they seek to evangelize and create a safe space for LGBTQIA+ people. At Trinity, they taught their congregation that when they bear witness to what is happening in the denomination, they also bear witness to those who fight for change within it. As youth witness the action for inclusion of their congregation, many of them are inspired to join the congregation as members, even as they believe the denomination is making a grave mistake in their decisions. The youth in all three of these congregations are active and empowered members of congregations and happily at odds with the denomination.

The Grace, Boston Avenue, and Trinity congregations do youth ministry differently than how it is often seen in mainline churches. These churches instead educate their young people about denominational polity and how decisions are made in order to change the doctrines

---

26 David Crary, "United Methodist Conservatives Detail Plans for a Breakaway," AP News, July 5, 2021, https://tinyurl.com/s26kbzrj.

in the church that are harmful to LGBTQIA+ people. These churches form, teach, and raise the youth to take their faith seriously, not only as a matter of personal piety, but also as those who organize for institutional change. They teach youth that when their faith leads them to disagree with their denomination, they must be public in their witness to this faith claim. These churches have taught their young people leadership and faith-based values of inclusion and love of neighbor. They have shown the youth how to bear out those values and love in action in the denomination and in their local congregations.

The importance of such choices cannot be overstated. Christian social ethicist at Garrett-Evangelical Theological Seminary, Kate Ott, and professor of practice at the Brown School at Washington University in St. Louis, Lorien Carter, argue that, "Creating a welcoming environment for teens of all sexual orientations and gender identities combats the sexual violence and harassment often experienced by teens."[27] I asked the adults I interviewed what they hope for their youth in the future. Paul said he wants the youth to know "that resistance but also conviction are spiritual disciplines and that there's room for those in any expression of church." In these churches, people of all ages are teaching, learning, and practicing these disciplines.

In 1987, Michael Warren, former professor of catechesis and practical theology at St. John's University in Jamaica, New York, published *Youth, Gospel, Liberation*, in which he argued that youth have inherited a legacy of silence.[28] Warren writes, "The lack of public voice of youth could also be called a political silence. Young people assume that they in fact can have no significant impact on the world."[29] Almost forty years since Warren's words, it is clear that silence is no longer the case in churches that have been educating their young people to exercise their agency in the church. Warren argued in his book that helping youth find and use their voice might happen well through involvement with social justice. These three churches have taught youth how they can make a difference and have walked beside them, encouraged them, and learned from them along the way.

---

27 Ott and Carter, "Revisioning Sexuality," 60.
28 Michael Warren, *Youth, Gospel, Liberation* (San Francisco: Harper & Row, 1987), 12.
29 Warren, *Youth, Gospel, Liberation*, 16.

There is increasing attention to organizing youth to be active in their communities for positive change. Teaching youth to organize as an act of faith is a concrete way to cultivate and empower young leaders to act for social change. Organizing gives them tools and empowers them to faithfully and tangibly respond to mistakes they see their denomination making. They might, as Peyton did, want to leave the denomination when they perceive the mistake to be egregious and at odds with their local church. They may instead decide to be confirmed in the denomination after witnessing the voices of those who choose to stay and fight for change from within.

Although none of the people I interviewed used the language of sin when talking about the UMC's former polity of exclusion, some of them spoke in such a way that showed they saw Sin at work. This was not the denomination "just" making a mistake. They objected to what the church had been doing because of their theology. The youth from Trinity who wrote the devotional saw that the denomination was excluding people whom God includes. The denomination had been acting in a way contrary to God. Michael, one of the youth at Grace, sees inclusion as consonant with Christian values he has learned through his Christian education at church, and exclusion as adhering to archaic norms and not those values.

In the youths' responses to the inequitable and harmful stance of the denomination, it is clear their theology is part of their perspective. Without using the term "sin" or categorizing the church as participating in the systemic Sin of oppression of a minoritized population, youth still interpreted based on these theological categories. There is room here to help youth tell it like it is, to call a sin a sin. This support might give youth more power as they attempt to speak into the new and inclusive future they hope for in the denomination.

In any case, youth formed and educated in churches that teach their youth principles of organizing are clearly empowered and leading change within their local churches and often in their schools and wider communities as well. The denomination had broken their hearts but not their spirits. They are faithful and strong leaders who are ready to do what Peyton said he sees as the responsibility of reconciling communities as the UMC goes forward: to make sure that whatever emerges from this transition will be as inclusive as possible.

Part Three

Navigating Sin and
Mistakes in Culture

CHAPTER EIGHT

The Color of Safety for Black and Brown Youth

Lakisha R. Lockhart-Rusch

Trigger warning: This chapter mentions rape, sexual assault, drug abuse, and police brutality.

"Put some pants on over those shorts until you get to the gym," shouted my mother from the other room. While I didn't understand why I needed to do so, I said, "Yes ma'am" and quickly threw on some sweatpants over my volleyball shorts. I knew better than to start an argument about something so small with my mother, even if I didn't agree. However, once I got to the parking lot of the school, I quickly took the pants off. After all, most of my other teammates didn't wear pants over their shorts—ever.

In the parking lot I saw some teammates, and we realized that we needed some tape to wrap our ankles. So we made a quick run to the store. None of us were wearing pants, just T-shirts and our volleyball shorts. However, I was the only one who got stares. An older Black woman came up to me and said, "Cover up, girl. You are practically asking for it. I know your momma taught you better than that." I ran out of the store in tears. I did not understand why someone would say something so mean—and only to me. What about my teammates who were wearing the exact same thing?

When I called my older sister, who had played basketball and volleyball when she was younger, to tell her what happened, she laughed. I still did not understand, but she was very clear that it was because I was

Black and I had booty. She told me that I filled out the shorts differently and I was expected to behave differently just because I was Black. She told me about her own experiences with being shamed and objectified and reassured me that it wasn't me. Rather, it was the way the world was.

I remember still being so hurt that my clothes could have possibly provoked certain attention or that I was "asking for it." I vividly remember my sister's voice as she got very serious and told me that I was not asking for anything. She told me it didn't matter if I had on shorts or if I was completely naked. I was not asking for anything, and I was not responsible for other people's actions, period. This was helpful, but still hurtful and confusing. I remember the feeling of guilt and shame that I had done something wrong—not just that I had made a mistake, but that I had somehow compromised my morals and ethics and had sinned against God.

As I grew older, I realized how much of what my sister said was true. My Black-girl body was often the subject and object of scrutiny, criticism, and unwanted attention. I was once told by an elder at church that my long-sleeve sweater dress that fell right above my ankles was too tight, showed my curves, and that I needed to dress less provocatively because I was tempting the young boys and the grown men. I was literally being told that my body in a dress was responsible for boys' and men's desire, lust, and sinful thoughts that might lead to actions. I was told the dress made me look "loose and fast" and that I was sinning before God for not carrying myself like a proper Proverbs 31 Christian woman of virtue.

I recalled my sister's words and asked the elder why I was responsible for the actions of boys or men. I also asked how my body in my dress was a sin before God—the same God who gave me this body, I thought. The elder quickly called me disrespectful and told me that if I continued dressing "loose and fast" and backtalking I would quickly be labeled a slut and, worst of all, God would not be pleased with all my sinning and making men lust after me and would let me get raped or hurt because I was not blessing God with my body.

As I grew older, the idea that how my Black-girl body was shaped and what I wore made me responsible for the actions of others being sinful continued. I experienced it at church when elders would speak to only the young girls and never to the boys about body shape and clothes, and pleasing God with our bodies, telling us that anything that was not saved for the man God would send us was a grave sin that would separate us from the love of God forever. I saw it on the news when newscasters would describe survivors of abuse or rape. Whenever the survivor was a girl or woman of color, news reports typically mentioned what she was wearing, what part of town she was in, or—worse—they would show a provocative or distasteful picture of her. For white female survivors, newscasters would typically display beautiful school or graduation pictures and mention a list of their volunteer work and future aspirations. I quickly learned that because of my body shape and race I would never be safe from unfair gaze, misjudgment, mistreatment, or the shame of sinning against God with my very existence in a Black girl's body. And neither are other girls and boys of color.

For many adolescents of color there is no safe space, just space to be bold, honest, open, and courageous in a world that often sees them as dangerous, criminal, and sexual objects. They rarely get to walk into a room without being misjudged because of their color. They rarely get to make mistakes without their race being a hindrance. There is scant safe space in the world or the church for adolescents of color and to name it as safe space is unhealthy, damaging, dishonest, and dangerous. Often youth of color are seen as problematic and sinful beings because their mistakes have much greater impact and effect on themselves and their communities. However, I have learned that these are just youthful mistakes—mistakes that we all make. The real sin is happening in the world and in the church when they promise safety that they cannot provide while perpetuating the mistreatment of Black and brown youth through white supremacy and racism. Youth must either internalize this to be "good Christians" or find other ways to respond that often take them away from the church that sees them and their being as the problem.

In this chapter, I look at and compare reported incidents and written materials of white adolescents and adolescents of color in order to understand and clarify why and how one racial group might be safer and able to make mistakes more than another. I offer practical suggestions to propose that all churches and spaces of religious education be places of prophetic voice in completely abandoning the notion and usage of safe space, which is only safe for a privileged majority, and move forward with creating a more sacred and creative space which encompasses dialogue, conflict resolution, honesty, vulnerability, mistake-making, and justice for all adolescents.

Black and Brown Girls

Objectification and oversexualization of girls of color often leads them to growing up far too soon or experiencing body shame or body dysmorphia, among other harms. Yet, many churches and classrooms still claim to provide safety when in fact they remain unsafe for girls of color. Even though viewing and treating girls of color like objects and property is documented in the Bible and many years ago during slavery, it still happens today. Not only does this happen in catcalls and cyberstalking, but in more physical and harmful ways such as rape and sexual violence, leaving one in five Black women having been raped in their lifetime.[1]

Girls of color not only experience physical harm from strangers, family members, and others they might know, but they can also experience another kind of physical attack—from the police. In 2015, neighbors called police with reports of a civil disturbance at a local pool party in McKinney, Texas. The police encounter started with a 911 call stating that teens were trespassing on private property and ended in Eric Casebolt, a former McKinney police officer, tackling—dragging and pinning down—Dajerria Becton, a fifteen-year-old Black girl wearing a swimsuit.[2] Casebolt was captured on video pulling the young girl by her braids and dragging her to the ground. After she was sitting on the ground, he then shoved her head against the grass twice. As she laid in the grass screaming for people to call her mother, the officer then

1 Carolyn M. West and Kamilah Johnson, "Sexual Violence in the Lives of African American Women: Risk, Response, and Resilience," VAWnet: The National Online Resource Center on Violence against Women, March 2013, https://vawnet.org/material/sexual-violence-lives-african-american-women-risk-response-and-resilience.
2 Dorothy A. Brown, "McKinney Pool Party Incident Has Everything to Do with Race," CNN Opinion, June 9, 2015, https://www.cnn.com/2015/06/09/opinions/brown-mckinney-pool-party/index.html.

placed his knees on the young, less than 100-pound Black girl's back and neck as she cried out in pain.[3]

The McKinney police chief Greg Conley publicly denounced Casebolt's actions, stating they were "indefensible" and did not reflect the "high standard of action" of his department.[4] The Becton family filed a civil rights lawsuit accusing Casebolt of using excessive and unnecessary force on the teenager.[5] From this lawsuit, the Becton family received $148,850, and $36,000 was divided among the six other teens involved in the incident.[6] Casebolt was placed on administrative leave and later resigned.[7]

This kind of dehumanizing disregard that happens when Black girls' bodies are seen by others as being in the wrong place at the wrong time or making/being a mistake is actually the sin that is being committed. Law professor Dorothy Brown stated it best in her CNN article: "This incident has everything to do with race."[8] If this girl had not been Black, this story would not have been a story at all because nothing would have happened. Black girls are not allowed to make mistakes without excessive and often disproportionate consequences, even when they are innocent. Dajerria's so-called mistake was existing in a Black girl's body. As a result, she was not safe and was the victim of the sin of white supremacy and racism.

Moving from physical harm to other instances of excessive and disproportionate consequences for mistake-making in Black girls and

3 Kristine Phillips, "Black Teen Who Was Slammed to the Ground by a White Cop at Texas Pool Party Sues for $5 Million," *Washington Post*, January 5, 2017, https://www.washingtonpost.com/news/post-nation/wp/2017/01/05/black-teenager-who-was-slammed-to-the-ground-at-texas-pool-party-sues-ex-cop-city-for-5m/.

4 Mira Oberman, "Texas Police Officer Who Pulled Gun at Pool Party Resigns," Yahoo News, June 10, 2015, https://mg.co.za/article/2015-06-10-texas-police-officer-in-pool-party-video-resigns/.

5 Phillips, "Black Teen."

6 Valarie Wigglesworth, "Attempt to Heal Rift over McKinney Pool Party Incident Turns into Heated Exchange between Activist, Mayor," *The Dallas Morning News*, May 29, 2018, https://www.dallasnews.com/news/2018/05/29/attempt-to-heal-rift-over-mckinney-pool-party-incident-turns-into-heated-exchange-between-activist-mayor/.

7 Ashley Southall, "Mckinney, Tex., Police Officer Resigns over Incident Caught on Video," *New York Times*, June 9, 2015, https://www.nytimes.com/2015/06/10/us/police-officer-in-mckinney-tex-resigns-over-incident-caught-on-video.html.

8 Brown, "McKinney Pool Party Incident."

women's bodies, I lift up US track star Sha'Carri Richardson. I will note that this situation happened when Richardson would technically no longer be considered a youth at twenty years old. However, given that Black and brown girls are often forced to grow up far sooner than they should, mentioning Richardson's situation still offers something for us to think about and consider in how the world treats and views Black girls' bodies.

Richardson failed her drug test before the 2020 Summer Olympics in Tokyo and was not allowed to compete. She tested positive for marijuana, which is not allowed, though it is not performance enhancing. Russian figure skater Kamila Valieva also failed a drug test but was still able to compete at the Beijing Winter Olympics in 2022.[9] The fifteen-year-old Valieva tested positive for trimetazidine, a banned medication that could increase endurance.[10] Richardson's mistake took away her opportunity to even compete, while Valieva's mistake did not. I will take a moment here to note that I believe the blame falls on unjust systems most of the time and not the young women. In this case, it is important to note that both Richardson and Valieva were deeply impacted by their personal decisions, and even more so by the systemic decisions of the International Olympic Committee. While Valieva was able to compete, putting a young girl in this kind of situation was unnecessary and unhealthy. Perhaps it was this stress that led to her falling during her skate and not medaling, when she was clearly the athlete expected to place high, if not win. This is only the physical toll that it took on her, I cannot even begin to imagine the psychological toll this took on both Valieva and Richardson. When these kinds of harmful decisions and injustices happen, more than just young Black bodies are harmed, but their psychological and mental well-being are greatly impacted.

Girls in Black and brown bodies are not safe and not allowed to make basic youthful mistakes without experiencing more drastic, unnecessary, and harmful consequences than girls in non-Black or brown bodies. Richardson's mistake was not only testing positive to a banned substance but doing so in a Black girl's body. She was not safe physically or psychologically.

---

9 Josephine Harvey, "Sha'Carri Richardson Notes 'Only Difference' She Sees between Her and Kamila Valieva," *HuffPost*, February 14, 2022, https://tinyurl.com/5ts5at6u.
10 Harvey, "Sha'Carri Richardson Notes 'Only Difference.'"

Black and Brown Boys

Let's say you do not inhabit a girl's Black or brown body, but a young boy's Black or brown body. Because of this, at some point you are at risk to going from being a cute, young Black or brown boy to being seen as a scary, dangerous criminal. "Black men are nearly six times more likely to be incarcerated than white men; Latino men are nearly three times as likely. Native Americans are incarcerated at more than twice the rate of white Americans."[11] The Bureau of Justice Statistics projected in 2001 that one in every three Black boys and one in six Latino boys born that year would go to jail or prison if trends continued.[12]

If you identify or appear to identify as a young Black or brown boy, you too are often more unsafe in many of these places that proclaim safety. While girls of color are often mistreated and abused, boys of color are often the first to be accused of something, physically harmed, and even killed. I have had adolescent Black and brown boys tell me stories about how everything was great in their church youth group until something went missing, and they were the first ones accused of being thieves and thugs—when they had done nothing. I have heard other stories of young boys who happen to inhabit Black and brown bodies being called dangerous, only good for sports, dumb, criminal, lazy, and a plethora of other things. When these young Black- and brown-bodied boys make "mistakes," they get the harshest possible punishment, whereas their white boy counterparts who do not inhabit Black and brown bodies are seen as smart, upstanding citizens that just had a youthful indiscretion and should be given volunteer work so as not to ruin the very successful life ahead of them. Because these young Black and brown boys often do not get the benefit of the doubt and do not have the same connections or funds that many of their non-Black and brown boy counterparts, the consequences for Black and brown boys' mistakes are frequently excessive, disproportionate, and sometimes deadly.

---

11 Jennifer Bronson and E. Ann Carson, "Prisoners in 2017," Bureau of Justice Statistics, April 2019, https://bjs.ojp.gov/content/pub/pdf/p17.pdf.

12 Equal Justice Initiative, "Racial Justice," accessed July 1, 2024, https://eji.org/racial-justice/.

While safety in the justice system can be flawed, there is often a presumed safety in neighborhoods and schools in which youth often walk and play, daily. You hear stories such as that of Trayvon Martin, who was brutally killed while his white Hispanic killer was acquitted. Then you hear the news stories of school killings where the killer is white and is simply captured and lives to fight another day, while an unarmed Black boy is shot multiple times or lays dead in the street for hours. The news is filled with these kinds of stories of white murderers getting acquitted because it was just a youthful indiscretion; Black and brown boys are just "thugs who deserved it." The news coverage even uses beautiful graduation and other appealing pictures of white perpetrators, while the coverage of stories about Black and brown bodies frequently uses very distasteful and criminal-looking pictures. Any "mistake" of just existing made by a boy in a Black or brown body is amplified with more hurt, more pain, more vitriol, and more death. Their mistake gets enlarged because of the sin of white supremacy and racism.

Elijah McClain was a twenty-three-year-old Black male who died three days after an encounter with the police on August 24, 2019, in Aurora, Colorado.[13] Police reports state that officers were responding to a 911 call about someone wearing a ski mask and flailing their arms, but who was not armed and no one was in immediate danger.[14] Once apprehended, officers left McClain on the ground for fifteen minutes. McClain was sobbing, vomiting, apologizing, and stating that he could not breathe. McClain's hands were cuffed behind his back and one of the officers had him in a carotid control hold around his neck. Officers said that McClain was acting erratically, so the paramedics injected him with ketamine. All three officers' body cameras came off during the incident, but the audio is available, and you can hear one officer tell the other to leave their camera on the ground. Originally, the autopsy and other evidence supported the claim that the officers did nothing

---

13 Lucy Tompkins, "Here's What You Need to Know about Elijah McClain's Death," *New York Times*, January 18, 2022, https://www.nytimes.com/article/who-was-elijah-mcclain.html.

14 "Elijah McClain Killing 911 Call & Police Body Cam Footage Transcript," August 25, 2019, https://www.rev.com/blog/transcripts/elijah-mcclain-killing-911-call-police-body-cam-footage-transcript.

wrong. However, after new evidence surfaced in a 2021 Grand Jury, the officers and the paramedic were indicted on thirty-two counts of manslaughter and criminally negligent homicide.[15]

Elijah was wearing a ski mask that night because he had a blood circulation disorder, and his arms were moving because he was listening to music and dancing.[16] His only so-called mistake was existing and daring to express Black-boy joy and he was killed for it. He was not just physically assaulted without cause, he was not only given drugs with no cause, but he was killed with no cause. He was killed for being a Black boy walking down the street. Elijah's "mistake" of existing in a Black boy's body cost him his life. He was not safe walking in a neighborhood. While these examples explore how Black and brown youth are unsafe in broader society, it is important to note that church spaces are a reflection of society. Church members work at schools and live in neighborhoods. It is churches that are often supposed to protect that end up perpetuating the sin of racism and white supremacy. We can and should do better.

What Can Religious Educators Do?

The biggest mistake that Black and brown adolescents often make is thinking that they are ever truly safe. That is a mistake, not a sin that should cost them their life and very belief in a God, community, or system that cares and protects them. They must live on guard and alert, and that fact is deplorable and sad, but it is the truth. These adolescents are not safe. As religious educators, we do not have to be complicit in allowing this to happen or creating space for this to happen without stopping it and naming it as wrong and sinful. There are many things that we, as religious educators, Sunday school teachers, youth ministers, parents, lay leaders, and church members can do too.

---

15 Eric Levenson, "Elijah McClain: Grand Jury Indicts Police Officers and Paramedics in 2019 Death of Elijah McClain," CNN, September 1, 2021, https://www.cnn.com/2021/09/01/us/elijah-mcclain-death-officers-charged/index.html.

16 Grant Stringer, "Unlikely Suspect: Those Who Knew Elijah Balk at Aurora Police Account of His Death," *Sentinel Colorado*, October 27, 2019, https://sentinelcolorado.com/news/metro/unlikely-suspect-those-who-knew-elijah-balk-at-aurora-police-account-of-his-death/.

Re-Name Space

Stop naming religious spaces as safe when they are not. Safe for or from whom? No space is ever really safe for everyone and to name it so is harmful, unhealthy, dangerous, and dishonest. It is time to stop lying, whether intentionally or unintentionally, to our youth about what we can and cannot do and why. We are not perfect and yet we pretend to be. Dare to be honest and vulnerable and name things as they are. Youth come to us with hope and trust that we are going to care for them, help them grow in faith, and be like Christ, but when we are dishonest, we break that trust and that hope. This breach in trust causes hurt and harm that will take a long time to heal if it ever does. Often, it is the lying and dishonesty that hurt our youth the most. In fact, to be able to proclaim safety can be a privilege for some.

Instead, have a conversation with your adolescents. Be honest about what can and cannot be provided in the space. Name that we are not perfect, and we all make mistakes. Name that we are flawed and human. Name that we will mess up, miss the mark, make a mistake, and so will they. Name this early and often and your youth will respect that honesty. Name that being dehumanized because of who they have been created to be in the world is wrong and a sin that they should not have to experience. Talk about having honest and hard dialogue, how you will deal with conflict when it happens, and how you will cultivate trust when someone is hurt. Then invite them to name the space for themselves. Maybe what they need and want is an open space, creative space, brave space, or maybe they still want to use the language of safe space, but let them do so with the knowledge of what can and cannot be provided within it.

Listen, Support, and Protect

Adolescents often have adult problems and concerns. Genuinely listen to them. Do not dismiss their concerns just because they seem trivial to you. Listen and stay present. Do not automatically go into fixing mode. Listen and ask what they might need, then offer support and protection when you can. However, I cannot stress the importance of listening fully and attentively first, so you can know how to best support and protect. Below is an example of a five-minute opportunity to put ourselves in the present moment by listening:

You start to listen well by first interrogating yourself. Don't feel you have to talk so much. If you can't hear other people, then you're taking up too much space. Take an inventory. Who's around you? Who is missing? Bring people in and genuinely listen.

Deeply listen even when it's not words. Deeply listen when I'm moved to tears and have no words. Deeply listen to this picture I have drawn, to this dance I create.

We are embodied people, with hearts and stories. You are someone talking to another embodied person, and how you deeply listen to them, and then are accountable to them, matters.

Because once you listen, you are deeply accountable. We will be held accountable to do the work together. This is the beautiful transformation for those that need to be heard and those that need to listen. It's the transformation that happens when we genuinely listen and see people for who they fully are, embodied in front of us.

This is important. This is life and death.[17]

Have Trainings

When was the last time you had implicit bias, racism, sexism, neurodiversity, mental health, and many other trainings to educate and equip your staff and volunteers to accompany Black and brown young people? Ensuring that your staff and volunteers are well trained and prepared is paramount. As staff and volunteers, we only have so much expertise and knowledge about certain things. It is okay to not know or understand or be good at everything. This is part of the being honest that was mentioned earlier. However, the good thing is that, if you do not know, you can ask professionals for help. Trainings led by professionals can help keep staff and volunteers be vigilant and can give them the necessary tools and resources to feel more capable in working with, knowing when to refer, and caring for adolescents.

This means not only training for safe sanctuaries and other mandatory training for the church and for adults to work with underage

---

17 Lakisha Lockhart, "Present Moment | Time to Listen: The Transforming Habit of Accountability," *In Trust Center Magazine*, Spring 2022, https://www.intrust.org/in-trust-magazine/issues/spring-2022/present-moment.

persons, but also other important things. Host training in intercultural competence, first aid and CPR, and implicit bias. Host training in bystander intervention, mental health awareness, and working with differently abled or neurodivergent persons. Host training about addiction, self-harm, and suicide awareness. The more you know about adolescents, the more you can help and reach them. Knowing the signs of danger or of an adolescent reaching out for help is important and can be the difference between life and death.

It is extremely important here to note that, just because we offer pastoral care, does not mean that we are licensed professionals, able to deal with all mental health issues that may arise. In fact, we are not, and often we can cause more harm by pretending we know more or can offer more help than we are able to. Start making connections now with various adolescent therapists, psychologists, and other helping agencies in your area. Have a coffee with a few addiction specialists or those who work with young girls and body image. The professionals are there, you just need to find them and build a relationship with them so that when your adolescents come to you, you can actually provide them the best care possible by sending them to someone who can truly help them. Begin to build a database of contacts and relationships, for the sake of your adolescents.

Additionally, knowing how to offer care and education to those that might be differently abled is vital. Knowing about accessibility ramps, places that do not have clearance for wheelchairs, places that have large spaces with echoes and make it difficult to hear are important things to consider prior to trips and outings. Having a plan of action already in place in case of emergency situations is also key. Start working on a crisis plan now.[18] The more prepared you can be in advance, the more likely you are to connect, keep that connection, and actually make a difference in the lives of adolescents.

Ditch Harmful Curriculum

Not all curriculum is created equal, and not all curriculum has the best interests of your adolescents in mind. Some curricula are tailored to

---

18 A helpful resource is Jessica Young Brown, *Making Space at the Well: Mental Health and the Church* (Valley Forge, PA: Judson Press, 2020).

more privileged groups and some are not as practical. Be sure you have a curriculum that not only represents your group culturally, but that also offers practical and helpful application for their lives, not just Bible verses to remember. Be sure your curriculum meets the needs of your group and that you have people that understand how to teach with it. If you cannot find one, create one. This is where a seminary or religious education course or two might come in handy, but, even if you don't have it, create it with the Holy Spirit and your group in mind. Start small by creating a theme for the month, then based on that create one lesson plan.[19] Then create another lesson plan, and then two more. You now have a month's worth of curriculum. Keep doing this until you have something for an entire year. You would be surprised what you can do with the experience, knowledge, and creativity that you, your staff, volunteers, and your adolescents have. Ask your staff, volunteers, and youth to help you create lesson plans. You will have that curriculum done in no time, and I am sure it will be amazing. If it goes well, consider publishing it or making it public (being sure to copyright and credit all contributors as necessary) on your church website for others to use.

Do the Work

Safety has a color, and it is not Black, brown, or rainbow. Remember that when you are working with adolescents. Remember that when you tell them the truth about being human and what you can and cannot provide. Remember that when you curate and name spaces. Remember to be sure that there is representation of your youth in the images on the walls, the music you play, and the food you prepare. Do your youth see themselves reflected in the space? If not, recreate and do it differently until they are represented and see themselves reflected and as made in the image of the divine. Invite them into the curation of the space, the images, the food, and naming process—let them tell you what they want and need.

---

19 There is a good lesson plan template in the book by Donald Griggs, *Teaching Today's Teachers to Teach* (Nashville: Abingdon Press, 2003).

When adolescents tell you what they need, remember to listen, support, and protect them. Presence is important to adolescents. They need people to hear them to life. To truly see them, even as they are still figuring out who they are. Be that person. See them. Hear them. Support them and protect them from others who would try to diminish their light and would perpetuate the sin of white supremacy and racism on their personhood.

By actively having training to educate and resource your staff and volunteers you are helping your adolescents to be seen, heard, and understood. Bring in other professionals to give you tools and resources and then keep their contact information. Start your network now. While these trainings can be expensive, try to get them written into your church's budget. Maybe you have a congregant who is already a professional and will offer services for free. Maybe professionals are looking for pro-bono work that can be a tax write-off. Maybe you can partner with another congregation that has a larger budget. Get creative; this is important.

Once you have all these great new tools and resources, use some of this new energy to find or create a curriculum that represents, reflects, and speaks to your adolescents. There are Christian education classes and certificates available at various seminaries and universities around the globe. Also, use your team and create curriculum together. You are the only people who know your youth and what they need. Know that you are enough to write curriculum for them, and you can do this for them. They are more than worth it.

Even though you cannot promise safety, there are so many other supports you can offer. Love, compassion, empathy, support, challenge, honesty, vulnerability, creativity, fun, laughter, a shoulder to lean on, an ear to listen, a body to stand in front of and protect them, pictures that represent them in their space—and the list goes on. Be aware, be intentional, and be proactive. Adolescents don't just deserve it; they need it.

CHAPTER NINE

When Consumer Culture Is the Mistake

Christopher J. Welch

Parents and other educators in faith often want the mistakes of youth to be learning opportunities, high-leverage moments that allow us to call on youth to reflect on their own actions as they relate to their identity and their relationships with God, self, and others. Mistakes and their correction can be part of a process of socialization, of coaching into habitual ways of acting and knowing that resonate with the gospel. Helping youth learn from mistakes is part of what religious educator Theresa O'Keefe names as the task of teaching youth to "navigate toward adulthood."[1] This understanding of the pedagogical value of mistake-making tends to operate on the assumption that adults themselves take ownership of a culture that is indeed good, that reflects the gospel. If there are mistakes, they are because youth have not yet adequately been socialized into this culture and have not fully learned its lessons.

However, when it comes to our culture of consumption, the problem is not that youth make mistakes that adults can help them to correct. Indeed, youth have been socialized into consumer culture all too well, generally with the unwitting complicity of the adults in their lives. The mistake is not in the learning. The mistake is in the culture itself. Religious educators, then, ought to problematize, for ourselves as well as for youth, consumer culture so that we can play a role in correcting

---

1 Theresa A O'Keefe, *Navigating toward Adulthood: A Theology of Ministry with Adolescents* (New York: Paulist Press, 2018).

that culture. Theologians have assessed consumer culture in light of the gospel and found the culture wanting. However, Christian educators have generally failed to respond pedagogically to meet the theological critiques of consumer culture in a way that brings more abundant life to the world. We must address that pedagogical and practical shortcoming.

Consumer Culture

Although there is some room for debate on just what constitutes culture and what indeed makes ours a consumer culture, few observers would fail to recognize US culture as consumerist. It is a culture deeply tied to economic systems and aspirations. As psychologist Helga Dittmar puts it, consumer culture can be seen as the "sociological and ideological manifestation" of late-modern capitalism.[2] In characterizing the dominant values of this late-modern capitalism, psychologist Tim Kasser notes an emphasis on self-interest, a strong desire for financial success, high levels of consumption, competitive interpersonal styles, and an orientation toward power and achievement.[3] In other words, consumer culture is a complex system of ideologies, structures, and practices that prioritize, at both personal and collective levels, competition, consumption, and self-interest. What marks consumer culture is not simply the sheer quantity of goods produced and consumed, nor even the seemingly insatiable desire for such goods. It is also the concomitant underlying belief that everything of value can be found in the marketplace.

Part of what has happened, though, is that this culture, which is humanly constructed, seems to be natural and immutable. What philosopher Charles Taylor calls the "social imaginary," the way a typical person in a society understands the world,[4] has been thoroughly

2 Helga Dittmar, "The Costs of Consumer Culture and the 'Cage Within': The Impact of the Material 'Good Life' and 'Body Perfect' Ideals on Individuals' Identity and Well-being," *Psychological Inquiry* 18, no. 1 (March 1, 2007): 23–31, https://doi.org/10.1080/10478400701389045.
3 Tim Kasser et al., "Some Costs of American Corporate Capitalism: A Psychological Exploration of Value and Goal Conflicts," *Psychological Inquiry* 18, no. 1 (2007): 1–22, https://doi.org/10.1080/10478400701386579.
4 Charles Taylor, *A Secular Age* (Cambridge, MA: Belknap Press of Harvard University Press, 2007), 171–176.

imbued with the values, principles, and assumptions of the consumer culture. Consumerism is not only normative; in most of our imaginations, there is not even an alternative. What we have, then, is a cultural poverty of imagination.

This impoverished imagination, indeed the culture of consumption as a whole, maintains its hegemony in part through the marketing that is so ubiquitous as to be almost unnoticed. Indeed, it is marketing that most effectively reproduces the culture in a way that purposely subverts critical consciousness, reflective discernment of the culture, and our place in it.[5] There is, then, an educative function to marketing. It offers us products and brand identities, but it also tutors us in desire. It taps into our desires, perhaps even creates our desires, but also teaches us what and how to desire. We are offered, in a sense, a catalogue of products, identities, and values into which we can imagine ourselves living—but not an infinite catalogue.[6] Marketing must train us to desire from among those choices. It involves an opening of (limited) possibilities, a tutoring in imagination, a formation of desire.

Such a culture is also most effective when transmitted early, and children and adolescents are among those socialized into some version of a consumer culture. From the perspective of those most invested in maintaining the culture, sociologist Norman Denzin describes the ideal child consumer as "a person who knows how to buy, wear, eat, watch, drink, and exchange cultural signifiers of childhood."[7] Child advocate Susan Linn,[8] sociologist Juliet Schor,[9] and others[10] have documented how marketing messages are aimed at children at younger

---

5 "The Persuaders," *Frontline*, November 9, 2004, http://www.pbs.org/wgbh/pages/frontline/shows/persuaders/.

6 Vincent Jude Miller, *Consuming Religion: Christian Faith and Practice in a Consumer Culture* (New York: Continuum, 2004).

7 Norman K. Denzin, "Foreword," in *Critical Pedagogies: Living and Learning in the Shadow of the "Shopocalypse"* (New York: Routledge, 2010), xiii.

8 Susan Linn, *Consuming Kids: The Hostile Takeover of Childhood* (New York: New Press, 2004).

9 Juliet Schor, *Born to Buy: The Commercialized Child and the New Consumer Culture* (New York: Scribner, 2004).

10 See *Consuming Kids: The Commercialization of Childhood*, DVD (Northampton, MA: Media Education Foundation, 2008).

and younger ages, so that branded characters and logos are part of their environment even from the cradle.

Unsurprisingly, exposure to consumer culture is causatively correlated with an assimilation of its values, what Kasser calls "materialism" that is both aspirational and dispositional.[11] While not all psychological studies of materialism utilize a single universal definition, L. J. Shrum calls materialism, "the extent to which individuals attempt to engage in the construction and maintenance of the self through the acquisition and use of products, services, experiences, or relationships that are perceived to provide desirable symbolic value."[12] The adoption of materialist values is symptomatic of "successful" socialization into consumerist culture. When adolescents act out the materialist values of consumer culture, they are not making mistakes; they are in fact living quite well what they have been taught, and it goes right to the core of their very identity.

Cause for Concern

The mere fact that consumer culture has achieved a dominance over our practices and our imaginations is not by itself problematic; what is problematic is that this culture causes significant harms on the personal, social, global, and ecological levels. Religious educators must be concerned not so much from the standpoint of finger-wagging culture cranks but as educators in faith in a God who desires the flourishing of God's creation. Christ stood with the suffering and wanted the rich young man not to go away sad but to follow him and live abundantly (Luke 18:18–23). Because in many ways consumer culture fails adequately to promote the common good and support human (and nonhuman) flourishing, we must educate for something better. Although the limitations of consumer culture are well documented elsewhere, this is worth a brief recapitulation here.

---

11 Tim Kasser, *The High Price of Materialism* (Cambridge, MA: MIT Press, 2002).

12 L. J. Shrum et al., "Reconceptualizing Materialism as Identity Goal Pursuits: Functions, Processes, and Consequences," in "Recent Advances in Globalization, Culture and Marketing Strategy," ed. Michel Laroche and Seong-Yeon Park, special issue, *Journal of Business Research* 66, no. 8 (August 2013): 1180, https://doi.org/10.1016/j.jbusres.2012.08.010.

Personal Harms

While every generation has its complaints about "kids today" being more materialistic, psychologists Jean Twenge and Tim Kasser argue that the complaint is empirically accurate, at least according to their longitudinal study between 1976 and 2007.[13] They tie those traits to both societal and personal insecurities, and so, while data on the levels of materialism among "Gen Z," those born between 1996 and 2010, are incomplete, we should certainly be attentive to the ways in which many Americans have experienced recent years as a time of uncertainty and insecurity. A global pandemic, partisan polarization, and national reckonings on racial disparities and sexual violence have made uncertainty part of the national mood for all age cohorts. Moreover, the corrosive effects of social media usage on the mental and emotional well-being of adolescents, particularly girls,[14] indicates that those uncertainties and insecurities may well be amplified by those media.

And it turns out that this materialism—which I am identifying as the internalization of the values of consumer culture—is correlated with ill-being. Psychologist Helga Dittmar has conducted an extensive meta-analysis of studies of materialism and well-being, variously defined and measured.[15] While she and her team noted some factors that seemed to exacerbate or mitigate the effects, well-being and materialism are strongly negatively correlated. Among the personal effects associated with materialistic values are depression, anxiety, narcissism, increased substance use, physical symptoms like headaches and stomachaches, and a lower frequency of the reported feeling of pleasant

---

13 Jean M. Twenge and Tim Kasser, "Generational Changes in Materialism and Work Centrality, 1976–2007: Associations with Temporal Changes in Societal Insecurity and Materialistic Role Modeling," *Personality & Social Psychology Bulletin* 39, no. 7 (2013): 883–897, https://doi.org/10.1177/0146167213484586.

14 Jean M. Twenge and Eric Farley, "Not All Screen Time Is Created Equal: Associations with Mental Health Vary by Activity and Gender," *Social Psychiatry and Psychiatric Epidemiology* 56, no. 2 (February 1, 2021): 207–217, https://doi.org/10.1007/s00127-020-01906-9.

15 Helga Dittmar et al., "The Relationship between Materialism and Personal Well-Being: A Meta-Analysis," *Journal of Personality and Social Psychology* 107, no. 5 (November 2014): 879–924, http://dx.doi.org.proxy.bc.edu/10.1037/a0037409.

emotions. These negative effects appear across a broad span of ages, but with particular force during adolescence.[16]

These negative effects seem to have accelerated as consumer culture has found expression with what the social psychologist and philosopher Shoshana Zuboff calls "surveillance capitalism." The elements of competition and comparison that have contributed so deeply to decreased well-being are, as most of us can readily understand, amplified when our very selves—created through our symbolic consumption and curated online—are always on display. The opportunities for increased levels of anxiety, depression, and body shame abound.[17] Paradoxically, this sense of always being on display and needing to be available to others seems to inhibit our ability to relate intimately and to increase our sense of isolation. We are in contact with more people, perhaps, but in genuine relationship with fewer.[18] The COVID experience simply highlighted a reality that was already emerging; we can drift through days communicating via text message, shopping entirely online (with twenty-four-hour delivery), and ordering food through a digital application that keeps us from ever actually interacting with another person. Our interdependence becomes invisible to us.

Social Harms

Beyond the negative effects of consumerism on individuals, especially on young people, there is concern about its social effects. Taylor has raised the concern that the individualism fostered by consumer culture furthers a complacency with privatized life and decreases civic participation.[19] Sociologist Robert Putnam has documented what he called the "collapse of American community."[20] In many spheres of public

---

16 Tim Kasser, "Materialism and Its Alternatives," in *A Life Worth Living: Contributions to Positive Psychology*, ed. Mihaly Csikszentmihalyi and Isabella Celega Csikszentmihalyi (Oxford: Oxford University Press, 2006), 200–214.

17 Shoshana Zuboff, *The Age of Surveillance Capitalism: The Fight for a Human Future at the New Frontier of Power* (New York: PublicAffairs, 2019), 445–474.

18 Sherry Turkle, *Alone Together: Why We Expect More from Technology and Less from Each Other* (New York: Basic Books, 2011).

19 Charles Taylor, *The Ethics of Authenticity* (Cambridge, MA: Harvard University Press, 1992).

20 Robert D. Putnam, *Bowling Alone: The Collapse and Revival of American Community*, rev. and updated ed. (New York: Simon & Schuster, 2020).

life, participation has decreased markedly. Both formal and informal participation in political and other forms of civic life have dropped off dramatically. He fingers a number of causes. One is the "work-and-spend treadmill" that leaves people working long hours to afford the goods that they want, and then wanting to use those goods in private.[21] This dearth of community connection tends to keep the poorest and most vulnerable poor and vulnerable, at significant cost to the society as a whole.[22] Materialistic pursuits crowd out both the time and energy for deeper personal relationships and for community involvement.[23] The wealthy can make up for a lack of community centers, public play spaces, and even adequate public education in a way that the poor cannot.

This enervation of community connections has the particular effect of isolating adolescents from integration in the whole of society. We as a society have created spaces for adolescents where the involvement of a small number of dedicated professional educators and coaches substitutes for the deep and wide practical concern of the whole proverbial village.[24] The problem is not that we have adolescents in high schools with professional teachers and with dedicated professional youth ministers on Sunday nights; the problem is that all too often we leave them only in high schools with professional teachers and only with the youth minister, and the guidance and wisdom of other adults in the neighborhood or church lie fallow.[25] Such analyses must be of concern for religious educators whose vision of social justice recognizes that the human person flourishes in a community, a community in which the broad participation of the many prompts a just distribution of the goods of that society.

---

21 See also Juliet Schor, *The Overworked American: The Unexpected Decline of Leisure* (New York: Basic Books, 1991).

22 Robert D. Putnam, *Our Kids: The American Dream in Crisis* (New York: Simon & Schuster, 2015).

23 Kasser, *The High Price of Materialism*, 61–62.

24 David F. White, *Practicing Discernment with Youth: A Transformative Youth Ministry Approach* (Cleveland, OH: Pilgrim Press, 2005).

25 John McKnight and Peter Block, *The Abundant Community: Awakening the Power of Families and Neighborhoods* (Chicago: American Planning Association and Berrett-Koehler Publishers, 2010), http://site.ebrary.com/lib/bostoncollege/docDetail.action?docID=10400822.

Global and Ecological Harms

Of course, the effects of the consumer economy on workers, especially in the developing world as employers "race to the bottom" for the lowest wages and loosest environmental regulations, have been part of the public conversation for decades.[26] Moreover, at least partly as a result of this consumption and the extractive attitude that underlies it, ecological disaster looms. Our consumption has already in many ways overshot the Earth's capacity to absorb it,[27] and, in another example of the market's failure to account adequately for matters of the public good, the effects of ecological overshoot fall disproportionately heavily on those who are already poor and vulnerable. This overshoot also, obviously, looms large in the present imagination and the future reality of today's adolescents. Climate anxiety is not an unreasonable reaction to the emergent ecological crisis, although it is also a costly one. A future of continuing climate change, resource depletion, economic shifts, and human displacement will impact today's adolescents for their entire lives. Such costs must enter the calculus of religious educators who prioritize practices of solidarity with the poor and vulnerable. Such realities must be of concern for those who educate in a faith that praises the God of all creation.[28]

The characteristics of consumer culture, then, are implicated in demonstrable personal, social, global, and ecological harm, especially to persons and communities that are particularly vulnerable. Because this culture is so naturalized as to be almost unnoticed, making it visible and challenging its hegemony is a pedagogical task, a task for those who, like Christian and other religious educators, are concerned with harm done to God's children and God's world.

The Flourishing Human Person in Culture

Underpinning all of the values of consumer culture, driving the processes that result in the exploitation of the vulnerable and the turn away

---

26 Naomi Klein, *No Logo*, 10th anniv. ed. (New York: Picador, 2009).

27 Juliet Schor, *Plenitude: The New Economics of True Wealth* (New York: Penguin Press, 2010).

28 Pope Francis, *Laudato Si'* (Vatican City: Vatican Press, 2015), http://w2.vatican.va/content/francesco/en/encyclicals/documents/papa-francesco_20150524_enciclica-laudato-si.html.

from the common good, is a malformed vision of what the human person is and what they are for. The critique of the late ethicist and Jesuit John Kavanaugh in his classic *Following Christ in a Consumer Society* still stands—at the root of consumerism is an anthropology that commodifies the person, makes them replaceable and marketable, and not valued in and for themselves. Human progress toward fulfillment is short-circuited, and their identity becomes swallowed up in consumption and materialism.[29]

Kavanaugh's hope for cultural change is grounded in a culture that values the human person as human person, not simply as a commodity.[30] This assertion then imbues humanity and human culture with theological and spiritual coloring. It is in this culture that humans continue to become who they are. In addition to their personal actions, they are both enabled and constrained by the culture in which they act. The culture, then, can facilitate or impede fulfillment, even as it is itself a human construct. As Karol Wojtyla (later Pope John Paul II) notes, "Man [sic] makes culture, needs culture, and through culture, creates himself."[31] What is at stake is not only action for personal flourishing but also the collective creation of the conditions in which people are most likely to flourish—the common good.

Evidence pointing to personal, social, and global ill-being indicates that consumer culture is not conducive to human flourishing. This cultural failure can be traced to the inadequacy of the anthropology that is operative in a culture of consumption. A culture grounded in a poor understanding of the human person is ill-equipped to foster the flourishing of that person. It is this misshapen culture into which adolescents are being socialized. If they are to flourish as individuals and to contribute to the common good, it ought to be in a differently shaped culture.

I assert here two lacunae in the operative anthropology of consumer culture, the culture of commodification. They are elements of the human person that are not adequately attended to in consumer culture, and their neglect exacerbates the harms of that culture. First, in

---

29 John F. Kavanaugh, *Following Christ in a Consumer Society: The Spirituality of Cultural Resistance*, 25th anniv. ed. (Maryknoll, NY: Orbis Books, 2006).
30 Kavanaugh, *Following Christ in a Consumer Society*, 75–87.
31 As quoted in Andrew N. Woznicki, *A Christian Humanism: Karol Wojtyla's Existential Personalism* (New Britain, CT: Mariel Publications, 1980), 44.

consumer culture, we imagine that the human person is not bound by our relationships of interdependence with other persons, by our creatureliness, nor by our embeddedness in the material world. We imagine ourselves to be "buffered" from dependence, intimacy, and finitude.[32] Community activists John McKnight and Peter Block call this condition the root of our "illusion of health, safety, comfort, and the like."[33] We believe we can expect order and consistency in our attempts to overcome suffering and loss, and in the existential quest for meaning. Other persons, societies, and the natural world are instrumentalized. We see them as valuable for how they contribute to our own quests for certitude.

Second, consumerism is built on and reinforces an anthropology that limits the person, as a consumer, to someone who makes meaning and identity only through the signaling they do with their consumption.[34] The rise of the brand economy is an especially egregious example of this anthropology. It is important to note, here, what the human person is *not*, at least not according to the operative anthropology of consumer culture. The person may be a laborer, but is not really much of a producer. What is produced is for the sake of consumption; there is no real production as creation.

The inadequacy of the anthropology of consumerism cries out for a fuller and better Christian anthropology. We need to imagine differently, more robustly, what the human person is. It is not enough that we move the human person back to the center of the culture, including the culture of consumption, if that culture is to be redeemed. We must also have an adequate conception of who that human person is, and what that human person is for, if the culture is to be truly humanized and therefore sanctified. The following aspects of such an anthropology are useful in considering the transformation of the culture of consumption: the person is relational; the person is a creative producer as well as a consumer; and the human condition is rightly subject to the constraints of finitude and creatureliness in a material world.

---

32 Taylor, *A Secular Age*, 2007.
33 McKnight and Block, *The Abundant Community*, 43.
34 Pierre Bourdieu, *Outline of a Theory of Practice*, trans. Richard Nice (London: Cambridge University Press, 1977).

A Relational Person

First, the human person is social and relational. Among the many contributions that feminist thought has brought to theology has been a thoroughgoing challenge to the modern conflation of personhood with isolation and individualism. Drawing on, but not limited to, the experience of women, feminist thinkers have helped to reclaim relationality as central to such fundamental elements of the human being as moral decision-making[35] and epistemology.[36] Postmodern philosophies of identity have challenged the monadic self that Charles Taylor claims "buffered" itself throughout modernity.[37] Indeed, the self is more and more seen to exist not *in se*, but only in relationship and negotiation with the persons, culture, and communities in which it exists.[38]

Relationality is part of the essence of the human person, as reflected in further theological insights pioneered or, rather, recovered by feminist theologians. In the Judeo-Christian tradition, it is foundational that humans are created in the image and likeness of God (Gen 1:27). Catherine Mowry LaCugna is among the theologians who have delved into the Christian doctrine of the Trinity and its implications for our understanding of the *imago Dei*. She emphasizes that the Trinitarian God is not simply three persons, but persons who are in relationships of giving and receiving, with each person of the Trinity absolutely needing the others; God is relational within Godself.[39] She writes, "The doctrine of the Trinity affirms that the 'essence' of God is relational, other-ward, that God exists as diverse persons united in a communion of freedom, love, and knowledge."[40] Such a claim compels us to consider human relationality not only as essential to our personhood but also as divine.[41] Because the project of human flourishing is about more fully

---

35 Carol Gilligan, *In a Different Voice: Psychological Theory and Women's Development* (Cambridge, MA: Harvard University Press, 1982).

36 Mary Field Belenky et al., *Women's Ways of Knowing: The Development of Self, Voice, and Mind* (New York: Basic Books, 1986).

37 Taylor, *A Secular Age*, 37–42, et seq.

38 Anthony Giddens, *Modernity and Self-Identity: Self and Society in the Late Modern Age* (Stanford, CA: Stanford University Press, 1991).

39 Catherine Mowry LaCugna, *God for Us: The Trinity and Christian Life* (San Francisco: HarperSanFrancisco, 1992).

40 LaCugna, *God for Us*, 243.

41 While there is a newness and freshness to this relational understanding of the Trinitarian God, it is also a recovery of what has long been part of the Christian

imaging God, then nurturing and being perfected in that relationality is part of the human task.

Catholic teaching has come to emphasize this social aspect of the human person particularly in light of the multiplication of social ties within and across societies that marked the second half of the twentieth century. The Second Vatican Council urged that this multiplication of social ties should also promote human development.[42] For John Paul II, this multiplication of social ties is the "interdependence" within which persons and societies are mutually formative.[43]

A social and relational anthropology (and concomitant theology) serves as a grounding for principles like the concern for the common good and the option for the poor and vulnerable. Without this understanding of the human person, these principles are somewhat arbitrary; with it, they are part and parcel of what it means to be human, to become most human. If the person is inherently social, then our life in common matters to the core of our very being and to Christian identity.

The Person as Creative Producer

Second, the human person is not only a consumer but also a creative laborer, a producer. Human labor is not merely for the production of what is to be consumed, but is an expression of human freedom and, in the understanding of John Paul II, an opportunity to participate in God's ongoing work of creation, to be cocreators with God. He sees work neither as a punishment for sin nor as an unfortunate consequence of humanity's fallenness, but as an essential, creative, and potentially sacred part of the human experience. The best of human work makes us "cocreators" with God. He distinguishes, though, between "work," which is creative and productive, and "toil," which is exhausting and minimally productive. Toil is indeed part of a fallen condition. A

Tradition. It was Augustine of Hippo who characterized the Holy Spirit as the personification of the love between God the Father and God the Son.

42 Second Vatican Council, *Gaudium et Spes*, 1965, 6, http://www.vatican.va/archive/hist_councils/ii_vatican_council/documents/vat-ii_cons_19651207_gaudium-et-spes_en.html.

43 Pope John Paul II, "Sollicitudo Rei Socialis" (Vatican City: Vatican Press, 1987), http://www.vatican.va/holy_father/john_paul_ii/encyclicals/documents/hf_jp-ii_enc_30121987_sollicitudo-rei-socialis_en.html.

culture of consumption that promotes sweatshop labor conditions—toil par excellence—is indeed a fallen culture, in need of redemption. [44]

Humans not only produce material goods, but also produce culture, even as we are shaped by that culture.[45] It was one of the goals of Brazilian educator Paulo Freire that people see themselves not simply as "subjects" of the culture but as "agents," and claim that agency.[46] This understanding of the human producing cultural objects and cultural meaning is part of an adequate understanding of the human person.

Embracing Finitude

The third aspect of a Christian anthropology that is essential to a healthy grappling with consumer culture is a recognition and even an embrace of human finitude. Finitude is not only a part of the human condition to be saved *from;* it is part of the human condition to be saved *in.* If sin is, at least to some extent, rooted in the self-aggrandizement that is an attempt to overcome the finitude of our mortality, our contingency, our "insufficiency unto ourselves,"[47] then there is something salvific in accepting and embracing this finitude.

It is this acceptance of finitude that the political theologian Johannes Baptist Metz describes as a disposition of "poverty of spirit," and embracing this finitude despite our longings to transcend it is indeed the very task of becoming more fully human. Of the incarnation, God's becoming human, Metz writes, "To become human means to become 'poor,' to have nothing to brag about before God. . . . Becoming human involves proclaiming the poverty of the human spirit in the face of the total claims of a transcendent God."[48]

Metz goes on to describe God's self-emptying into a Christ who was truly human, truly poor in spirit, as the model of humanization.

---

44 Pope John Paul II, "Laborem Exercens" (Vatican City: Vatican Press, 1981), http://w2.vatican.va/content/john-paul-ii/en/encyclicals/documents/hf_jp-ii_enc_14091981_laborem-exercens.html.

45 Kavanaugh, *Following Christ in a Consumer Society,* 80–84.

46 Paulo Freire, *Pedagogy of the Oppressed,* trans. Myra Bergman Ramos (New York: Continuum, 1970).

47 Johannes Baptist Metz, *Poverty of Spirit,* rev. ed. (New York: Paulist Press, 1998), 25.

48 Metz, *Poverty of Spirit,* 10.

"Christ showed us," he says, "how to really become human beings."[49] Becoming most fully human is to be liberated from "slavery" to the anxiety brought on by a rejection of finitude; it is to be liberated "obediently accepting our innate poverty."[50] Our limitations, our materiality, our finitude are part of who we are.

As for the shape that society moving toward liberation takes, then, it is a society that promotes the common good, cares especially for the poor and vulnerable, attends to the natural limits of our created world, and catalyzes the flourishing of human persons who are creators as well as consumers, who grow in relationship and in community, and who are able to find joy in the paradoxes of freedom and finitude.

More prosaically, embracing finitude highlights not only the limits but also the possibilities of our materiality. Philosopher Matthew Crawford has noted that materialism in consumer culture, ironically, often leaves us divorced from the realities of the material world and our own participation in it.[51] It enables a narcissism that draws on an assumption that we can technologize or buy our way to mastery. In this "delusion of omnipotence," the world is an extension of our own will.[52] Pope Francis similarly writes of the "technocratic paradigm" as a mindset that allows humans to treat the natural world as if it has no limits, or as if humankind can transcend the limits of the material world through the magic of technology.[53]

Practices for a Culture of Human Flourishing

Bikes for Change (BfC)[54] is a community-based organization in a northeastern city. Its mission statement proclaims that it sees the bicycle as "a vehicle for social change." On this day, their workshop space

---

49 Metz, *Poverty of Spirit*, 19.

50 Metz, *Poverty of Spirit*, 28.

51 Matthew B. Crawford, *The World beyond Your Head: On Becoming an Individual in an Age of Distraction* (New York: Farrar, Straus & Giroux, 2015).

52 Matthew B. Crawford, *Shop Class as Soulcraft: An Inquiry into the Value of Work* (New York: Penguin Press, 2009), 16.

53 Pope Francis, *Laudato Si'*, 106–109.

54 Both the name of the organization and the names of any persons mentioned have been changed. Research at BfC was subject to the Boston College Institutional Review Board's approval for the protection of human subjects.

is crowded with a dozen teens nearing the completion of the six-week Earn-a-Bike course. Teens have spent three hours a day in the program, learning about safe cycling and bike mechanics, but also some lessons about community development and power. At the end of the six weeks, each participant brings home a bike that he or she has, with staff help, refurbished.

If part of what is problematic about consumer culture is its truncated and inadequate anthropology, BfC, as a "community of productive practice" with an emphasis on youth, points to three particular ways in which its ethos and ideology can help point to a repersonalization that fosters integral humanism with the goal of human flourishing. This repersonalization takes place in a space that engages youth in grappling with their relationality, the finitude of their materiality, and their role as creative producers and not only consumers. It is a space where newness in practice encourages youth and adults alike to consider new ways of being, to enhance their imaginations. BfC offers a space for the resistance that is part of the process that Old Testament scholar Walter Brueggemann calls the prophetic task, where grief and resistance can lead to new hope.[55] While BfC is in no way a faith-based organization, the church must always be attentive to opportunities to notice and learn from God's work throughout society. Observation of the experience of participants at BfC and interviews with youth point to some elements that religious educators can use in helping ourselves and our young people to re-form our mistaken, acritical acceptance of a culture of consumption in the service of personal and cultural transformation.

Finitude and True Materialism

First, BfC offers a space for a grappling with and respect for the finite possibilities of the material world. At BfC, the practices of bicycle repair and the discourse around those practices tend to foster what sociologist Juliet Schor calls a "true materialism" that entails a valuing of our material products commensurate with the natural and human costs of their production.[56]

---

55 Walter Brueggemann, *Reality, Grief, Hope: Three Urgent Prophetic Tasks* (Grand Rapids, MI: Wm. B. Eerdmans, 2014).
56 Schor, *Plenitude*, 119.

For instance, nineteen-year-old Daniel was a participant in the BfC youth program who then became employed there part-time as an instructor in that program and then in their affiliated bike shop. He noted that, busy with his job, he had neglected his own bike recently, which was going to require some significant work to get it running well. His intention to rebuild it was a matter of aesthetics, a sense of ownership, and an appreciation for the material reality of the bike. Repair and restoration are symptoms of his "true materialism." He said:

> I mean, I would modify it, to improve it, but, I don't know, it's just like that bike, it's just like, I've had it for so long and I love the way it is and how it rides and stuff. . . . But it's just, I love the bike so much, I don't want to just let it go to waste and let it break down. I just want to keep it for as long as possible. And I built it.

Part of what seems to make this shift to true materialism more likely seems to be the practice of repairing the bicycles. On one occasion, a fourteen-year-old boy struggled to fix his brakes—a process that can take quite a bit of trial and error when aligning the pads to the braking surface of the wheel. As he worked, he expressed a mixture of pride, anticipation, and frustration. At one point, in the midst of a tricky part of the repair, he dropped his tools in exasperation, growling, "I want to be done right now!"

This experience, says Matthew Crawford, "chastens the easy fantasy of mastery" that permeates the culture of consumption. Instead, the repairer has to "notice things" for what they are, get into the reality of the material world. They cannot simply impose their will on the machine as they imagine it to be, but must work with it as it is, must figure out how it has worn, what is not working and why, and often craft repairs based on what materials are available rather than according to an idealized manual.[57] The practices of repair and maintenance force us to confront not only the limits of the materials with which we work but also our own limits. As an antidote to narcissism, the practice of repair also allows us to accept and even to embrace finitude. We cannot have everything, buy everything, do everything, and be everything.

---

57 Crawford, *Shop Class as Soulcraft*, 17.

Relationality and Respect for Persons

Second, and related, if BfC offers a space for the true materialism that rejects a culture that easily disposes of objects, it similarly fosters, quite intentionality, a relationality that resists a culture that would do the same to persons. Deron, who graduated from the program and then went on to work there, said that what drew him more deeply into the program was really the people, the instructors who were always willing to help and to teach him something extra. Sheila, too, noted that, while she been involved at BfC in different roles over a number of years, what drew her in and kept her so long was the sense of respect she felt from and for others.

Such an atmosphere does not simply or automatically happen at a place like BfC; it must be maintained intentionally. A contract of rules signed on the first day of the program by the participants and hanging on a door lists "No bullying," "Respect," and "Be nice" among the precepts. Another poster in the workshop proclaims BfC a "No Joke Zone." The point is not that humor is not permitted—in fact, I observed a generally chatty and jovial atmosphere. It is to eliminate the bullying or harassment that often slides under the radar as humor. Deron cited this particular rule as essential to the ethos of BfC, and his language indicates that he has been steeped in it. It empowers people to stand up for themselves. As he put it: "You don't have to explain yourself why you don't like the joke, you just say that and it's automatically supposed to stop. And that really, really helps people because that really curbs the amount of, if there was bullying, it would curb that. But there's not bullying just because of simple rules like that."

Daniel captures this synergy between respect for the material world and respectful relationships with persons in his own poignant story. As someone who experienced difficulties with learning in school, he started in a BfC program with others with learning disabilities, having little confidence in his ability to learn. When he learned mechanics, he began to see himself as a learner and a doer. What first got him to stay involved at BfC was the opportunity to teach youth like himself. "Seeing kids like that learn, and being able to do it, is very impressive. And it shows . . . how much potential they have." When I asked him if he saw a connection between his desire not to waste a good bike and his desire to make sure kids with disabilities get a chance to feel the freedom he feels when riding a bike he built, Daniel nodded his head in vigorous agreement.

Agency and Producers

Third, in an age when so much about our worlds has been designed keep us ignorant of the reality, to deskill us, in fostering something as straightforward as the "manual competence"[58] of bicycle repair, BfC helps to cultivate a sense of agency in the person as not simply a consumer but also as a creative producer. In the process, BfC opens up the possibility for greater self-efficacy in other areas as well.

Certainly, the sense of efficacy one derives from what Crawford calls "manual competence" is hard to deny. A favorite moment of mine at BfC came when one of the youths completed a brake repair about which he had expressed anxiety and on which he had spent considerable time. As he grasped both brake levers and realized that the repair was done, and done well, he clenched his jaw and said, "Yes! Did it! Like that!" He was, it seemed, pleased not only at the mechanical result but also, even more so, with his unfolding identity. He was a repairer, a producer, and it mattered to him. Another pair of participants, after completing their bike repair, conversed about hacking their smartphones to use on different networks. Their sense of agency, it seemed, was growing and spilling over into other domains.

This efficacy as a creative producer seemed to bleed into other areas as well, into a sense of self as producer of culture. As with respectful relationships, this element of BfC was intentional. Deron spoke about the way his work at BfC gave him confidence and voice. Malik, though he claimed not to know anything about politics when he came to BfC, told me that he had learned about gentrification there, and then headed out to lead a street rally protesting a newly proposed housing development. Sheila noted what she called an "A-ha" moment, when she realized that her mechanical skills led to her teaching others, gaining confidence, and taking on a role in an industry where African American women have few prominent places. In other words, it was hard not to see the goals of developing cultural and mechanical agency coming together at BfC.

---

58 Crawford, *The World beyond Your Head.*

Educating for Interdependence, Creativity, and Reflective Practice

Interviewing and observing participants in the BfC program suggests some ways in which religious educators might take seriously our charge to socialize youth into a better culture, a culture more conducive to human flourishing than is the culture of consumption. We must, of course, adapt these ideas for our own circumstances—one size does not fit all. Still, I suggest that we consider implementing some of the practices at BfC in the context of religious education spaces.

First, we should be intentional about the environment and culture in which youth meet and work together so as to foster relationships of interdependence. Faith-based schools, sacramental preparation programs, and youth groups often feature community service requirements and opportunities. Simply doing something for others is, inherently, a good thing. Facilitating thoughtful reflection on this service enhances the learning experience. However, the content and structure of these service opportunities could, when appropriate, be tailored to help youth develop in line with an anthropology that fosters human flourishing.

One way to leverage community service projects and other sorts of experiential learning to engage youth is to emphasize their dependence on each other. For instance, developmental psychologist Robert Kegan describes a vocational education program whose greatest success, as he sees it, is the way it socializes its participants into understanding and valuing their relationships with others. The program happens to teach boat-building, but the activity almost does not matter; what matters is that it is structured in such a way that participants' work depends on others doing their work. Participants report being aware of their dependence on others and, perhaps more importantly, of caring that others depend on them.[59] If we put youth into community service and experiential learning projects where they become aware of classmates and of community members who are depending on them, and where they depend on the work of classmates and community members in order to make their own contribution successfully, they are in a better position to understand their interdependence with others.

---

59 Robert Kegan, *In Over Our Heads: The Mental Demands of Modern Life* (Cambridge, MA: Harvard University Press, 1994), 46–47.

In addition to structuring activities such that youth become aware of their interdependence with others, we must create in our religious education classrooms and youth groups spaces that allow persons to flourish in relationships. It is generally the case that Christian educators bring their best selves and genuine care to their work with youth, such that by the sheer force of good example they create a culture of respectful relationship. It is especially gratifying when, in these religious education spaces, we see the blossoming of relationships that might not have grown outside of this milieu. We have probably all, however, also found ourselves in situations where our best hopes for a culture of caring relationships among youth is subverted. Our care and concern do not automatically overcome the relational barriers that our youth experience in other aspects of their lives together. BfC's explicit attention to the social and emotional elements of their program reminds us that we may need to supplement our infectious care with intentional development of those relationships. What is in the air, on the walls, and structured formally and informally into norms in the class or group cannot simply be left to chance. Even in the physical environment of our spaces of religious education, we can make explicit the norms and expectations that promote growth in relationships.

Second, we should allow youth to be creative producers in the material world. For instance, it is not uncommon that the community service performed by religious education classes and church youth groups includes engagement with the possibilities and frustrations of the material world. Youth participate in home-building and repair projects, community gardening, and cleaning. So, we should find avenues for youth to participate in this sort of work that forces them to confront the limits and possibilities of the material world. In fact, this creative production need not be limited to service projects. Youth activities in the church can sometimes simply involve fun productive activities—crafts, art, or hobbyist skill-building. However, the lessons about materiality—both the true materialism championed by Schor and the identity of youth as creative producers—are best learned when they have the opportunity explicitly to reflect on these experiences. Let us put our youth in a position to do and to reflect on that doing.

Third, we must help youth engage in reflection on and experimentation with their relationship with consumer culture. Because consumer culture is so ubiquitous and its assumptions seem natural, Christian educators can undertake the task of helping youth make the invisible visible. In fact, it is not uncommon for youth to have some inkling that there is something unsatisfying about their experience of consumer culture, but they find it hard to name at first. Christian educators can help them identify just what consumer culture is, how it influences them, and maybe ask them to consider how they actually want it to influence them. Only then might they imagine living into alternatives—not only alternative practices, but alternative identities, identities that are broader and deeper than those offered them in the culture of consumption, identities befitting children of God living life abundantly.

As much as we all sometimes forget it in the dailiness of work with youth, they are tremendously adept at the task of being socialized into the culture. When that culture itself is inadequate for the promotion of the common good and of the flourishing that is God's dream for us, our mistake is in failing to interrupt that socialization. We ought to promote for youth socialization into a culture that takes seriously human interdependence, values the material world, and fosters creative production. While organizations like Bikes for Change offer examples of why and how to invite youth into such a culture, as a church we can draw on these examples in ways that can be adapted to the particular strengths of our institutions and the gospel's call to promote the life of abundance.

Conclusion

May It Be So

Cynthia L. Cameron, Lakisha R. Lockhart-Rusch, and Emily A. Peck

We conclude where we began: teenagers are fundamentally good. They *already embody the fullness of humanity*. They are good because God created them good. They must be seen in the fullness of their humanity. The church must not dismiss them as not-yet-adults, as only the "future of the church" (rather than its present), or as simply awkward and rude children. They have gifts by virtue of being teenagers and are an essential part of the Body of Christ. And they will make mistakes. They will also sin. Both are part of our shared human experience. Teenagers are, like all of us, formed by the communities they belong to and by the Spirit working in their lives.

There is a fine line in Western culture, and maybe particularly in US culture, between personal responsibility and letting others off the hook. In an episode of the podcast *On Being*, journalist Ezra Klein offered his analysis, saying:

What are the structures that shape people's decision-making? What are the structures that lead us to be who we are? I think that we often have an illusion that we made a choice for ourselves, when that choice was so fundamentally shaped by who we are and where we grew up and what was around us and what made sense for us to do, that in some final accounting, it was really almost never a choice at all. And I think

> when you look at the world like that, then it becomes very, very deeply
> important—it becomes of central importance—that those systems are
> just and that, in some big way, we are helping people who were born
> into, or who fell into, the wrong systems.[1]

Upon close inspection, churches, schools, and youth ministries might find that they inadvertently uphold an individualist, autonomous ethic of personal responsibility when they teach youth that they must take care not to make mistakes, or worse, that the mistakes they are bound to make are the same as sinning. We may be teaching our young people that they are in control of a lot more than they actually are. They cannot control systemic racism. They cannot control rampant consumerism. What they can do is learn how to look at the world and their choices in a theological way, learn how to recognize the ways that their choices are shaped by the culture, and, when appropriate, name it as it is: Sin.

Sin with a capital "S" is often how Paul talks about it. For example, in Romans 6:17, Paul writes, "But thanks be to God that you, having once been slaves of Sin, have become obedient from the heart to the form of teaching to which you were entrusted." He knows that Sin can enslave humanity, can take away our freedom. He also knows that, "if anyone is in Christ, there is a new creation" (2 Cor 5:17). Have we done enough to teach our youth that sin no longer controls us and we are new in Christ? Have we done enough to teach our youth that being new in Christ doesn't exempt someone from making mistakes or from sinning, but it does provide us with a community with whom we can wrestle with the difficulties of living as new creations in an old world. We can surround ourselves with a community rooted in hope and always seeking to act in ways consistent with the expectation that our hope can be fulfilled: the fully realized kin-dom of God.

The authors of this book want to be part of teaching youth that mistakes are a part of life and help us in our growth and formation. We want youth to learn that mistakes and sins are not the same thing, and further, we want youth to know that if some people seem to be allowed to make mistakes and others are not, then systemic Sin is probably at

---

1 Krista Tippett and Ezra Klein, "How We Walked into This and How We Can Walk Out," *On Being with Krista Tippett*, February 6, 2020, https://onbeing.org/programs/ezra-klein-how-we-walked-into-this-and-how-we-can-walk-out/.

work. We want our youth, the adults who work with them, live with them, love them, and, indeed, all Christians to be able to identify where systemic Sin is present and be part of taking away its power. We want them to know when they have made mistakes that require the acknowledgment of wrongdoing and the attempt to heal relationships. We also want them to know that neither their faith communities nor God's grace abandons them when they sin. We can do this through seeing, respecting, empowering, and responding to the embodied fullness of humanity of youth. Ashe. Amen. May it be so.

Epilogue

Youth Are the Church, Not the Future of It

Patrick B. Reyes
Dean, Auburn Theological Seminary

What do you do when the world wants you dead?

Chicano poet and author Jimmy Santiago Baca writes from the experience of being incarcerated in his youth. His words are medicine for a generation of youth, young people, and the young at heart who have been marked for dead. In his books of poetry and memoirs, he invites the reader to imagine a world where Chicano and Apache youth have been discarded. Despite this reality, he challenges readers to look for beauty and imagine a full life in community.

Cameron, Lockhart, Peck, and the collected authors offer an invitation not unlike Baca's. What do we do as Christian religious educators as we sit between youth who have been left out, marginalized, labeled a mistake, a problem, or seen as living in sin, and the institutional church?

The unwavering commitment to exploring the experiences of youth at the margins—LGBTQIA+, racial-ethnic minorities, and others whose identities have pushed them outside the Christian church—allows for one of the most honest, raw, and revealing religious education anthologies to emerge in the last two decades.

I returned to Baca's poetry as I read *Nobody's Perfect*. His mystical poetry grounded me in the imagination of youth—something I longed for as I read this book. His poem "Who Understands Me but

Me" follows what youth on the margins are experiencing.[1] In each line, he explores what it means to be a youth discarded by society—locked in a cage, where food, water, and community are withheld. He writes about a place so void of joy that tears were hard to come by. He writes what to do without family, without freedoms, to live in a place without the agency to experience the divine.

And yet . . .

His response to this space is not just to find and search for beauty but to recognize it is there. His call, a call to the authors collected here, is that youth will find and make beauty because the Spirit is with them. God's Spirit dwells in and with them. Youth look inside and imagine a world beyond the violence they have been dealt.

If youth so pushed to the brink can make beauty in these conditions—when they should not have to—why are adults and leaders of the church not following and learning from their ability to imagine? Or perhaps, a better way to put it: Why are so few beyond the mystics and prophets among us able to see youth as the church?

While much of *Nobody's Perfect* reflects on how the church has marginalized youth, there are glimmers of hope. What if the imagination of the youth themselves shaped what it means to be community? It is precisely in a young person's soul, mind, and body that the church finds its ministry.

What is in the way of us realizing this ministry? Sin. Sin is a failed imagination to see youth as fully human. While the authors offer a challenge the way the church has leveraged sin against youth, I want to offer a different frame.

The question I ask following my own Chicano upbringing is counter to the formation explored or challenged in this book. What if we took Baca's invitation to find and make beauty with youth in the borderlands as the central task of ministry? Or better, how might I better sin with them, to learn alongside them? I go where the sinners go. What must we risk in the present—failed notions of Christian purity and who has authority in the church—to gain a thriving future—an expansive imagination guided by young people's lives? How can I sin as they do?

---

1 Jimmy Santiago Baca, "Who Understands Me but Me," accessed July 2, 2024, https://www.poetryfoundation.org/poems/53093/who-understands-me-but-me.

Each author has invited us to see the way the church, in living into its vocation, fails its first believers. They invite us to see how religious educators can reimagine following those who first followed Jesus: youth.

Inspired by this book, I want to invite us who may be young at heart, in soul, and in mind, but not young in body, to reimagine our witness and ministry in three moves.

1. Make beauty with, not for.
2. Youth are the church now, not the future of it.
3. We need elders.

Make Beauty

Religious educators need to make beauty, be inspired by it, sponsor it, pay for it, and be led by it. Youth are not just to be pastored to, in need of my or your wisdom—at least not at first. What they need is someone to be present to their dreams and imaginations. They need leaders to be curious about how they make meaning. They need leaders to make beauty with them.

Youth Are the Church Now, Not the Future of It

If there is one thing that this book has made clear it is that youth need to be seen as fully human. They are not a program or problem to be fixed. Taking it a step further than the contributions suggest, youth are the church. We need to center their experience and imagination about and for the world. They are our pastors. We can offer resources as they explore what ministry looks like, but let us not try to imagine that Jesus's ministry was to go out and try to convince the religious establishment. In fact, our move to center youth should agitate those in power. Anything less would be to fail to follow Jesus and the youth with whom he entrusted a movement.

We Need Elders

I go to bed early because I am tired. I am no longer young in body. But my research shows the age of my body matters very little for my role in how young people find meaning and purpose. They find it through relationships with elders who have spoken their gifts and are inspired by those just a little further in the journey. Yes, they have dreams and imaginations. And we need to imagine that living fully into our calls, pursuing a healed world, making beauty, or just breathing despite the world trying to cast us aside inspires young people to keep going! Every time a poet like Baca reads poetry that resonates with a young person's soul or an artist sings lyrics that reflect their passions, or a grandma, auntie, teacher, coach, or pastor lives fully into their vocation, young people see a version of themselves. Inspire with how you live your life. Young people desire to be in relationship with people who inspire them!

Make beauty. Youth are the church. We need elders.

If I had to gesture to volume 2 of this anthology, it would be to follow Baca's invitation. How can we make beauty with, not for, youth? How do we center youth as the church, not the future of it? How do we engage as elders?

The answer to this invitation is not difficult. Just do it! As elders, we can sponsor the album, the chapbook, the curriculum, the art, and the ministry of young people. To all those young people who have been marginalized by the institutional church, I sincerely wonder if those of us who believe the Spirit is already with them will have the courage to stop telling the institution it messed up and start to embody a ministry and teaching that follows the Spirit. To the authors of this work, I express my gratitude to pointing the reader to where the Spirit is, and I take your invitation as a call for the church to be the church. To close let me offer a blessing and invitation:

To the Divine of My Ancestors,

How I long for the days when my heart was on fire
When I knew I could change the world
When I knew I could change myself
If someone would just give me a chance

How I long to be seen, heard, valued, and loved
When I knew abuse to this body was not okay
When I knew I could survive it
Asking God to let me breathe just once more

How I long for the days when love stirred my spirit
When I was certain of what was right
When I was certain I got certainty wrong the next day
Crying out for someone to love me

How I long for another rite of passage
When the community recognized my move from youth to adulthood
When one day I was ready for the change
And then next was hoping for a return of childhood

How I long for my friend to return to me
When they were taken too long
When my innocence was stolen from me
Hoping it would return through the love of my elders

How we long for the youth to lead
When they have the love of the ancestors
When their imagination makes room for our descendants
Living into what ministry can and should be

The youth are the church
May we have the courage to follow

Selected Bibliography

Althaus-Reid, Marcella. *Indecent Theology: Theological Perversions in Sex, Gender, and Politics.* London and New York: Routledge, 2000.

Atwood, Craig D. *The Theology of the Czech Brethren from Hus to Comenius.* University Park: Pennsylvania State University Press, 2009.

Baard, Rachel Sophia. *Sexism and Sin-Talk: Feminist Conversations on the Human Condition.* Louisville, KY: Westminster John Knox Press, 2019.

Baker, Dori Grinenko. *Girl/Friend Theology: God-Talk with Young People.* Cleveland, OH: Pilgrim Press, 2023.

———. "Love Letters in a Second-Hand Hope Chest: Working-Class White Girls Delaying Dreams and Expanding Soul." In *The Sacred Selves of Adolescent Girls: Hard Stories of Race, Class, and Gender,* edited by Evelyn L. Parker, 107–129. Cleveland, OH: Pilgrim Press, 2006.

Baker, Dori Grinenko, and Joyce Ann Mercer. *Lives to Offer: Accompanying Youth on Their Vocational Quests.* Cleveland, OH: Pilgrim Press, 2007.

Belenky, Mary Field, Blythe McVicker Clinchy, Nancy Rule Goldberger, and Jill Mattuck Tarule. *Women's Ways of Knowing: The Development of Self, Voice, and Mind.* New York: Basic Books, 1986.

Berryman, Jerome W. *Children and the Theologians: Clearing the Way for Grace.* New York: Morehouse Publishing, 2009.

The Book of Discipline of the United Methodist Church, 2016. Nashville: The United Methodist Publishing House, 2016.

Bourdieu, Pierre. *Outline of a Theory of Practice.* Translated by Richard Nice. London: Cambridge University Press, 1977.

Brown, Jessica Young. *Making Space at the Well: Mental Health and the Church.* Valley Forge, PA: Judson Press, 2020.

Brueggemann, Walter. *Reality, Grief, Hope: Three Urgent Prophetic Tasks.* Grand Rapids, MI: Wm. B. Eerdmans, 2014.

Brumberg, Joan Jacobs. *The Body Project: An Intimate History of American Girls.* New York: Vintage Books, 1997.

Bussey, Kay, and Albert Bandura. "Social Cognitive Theory of Gender Development and Differentiation." *Psychological Review* 106, no. 4 (1999): 676–713.

Cameron, Cynthia L. "You Are the Now of God: *Christus Vivit* and the Need for a Theological Anthropology of Youth." *Horizons* 50, no. 1 (June 2023): 110–135.

Cheng, Patrick S. *Radical Love: An Introduction to Queer Theology.* New York: Seabury, 2011.

Clark, Chap. *Hurt 2.0: Inside the World of Today's Teenagers.* Grand Rapids, MI: Baker Academic, 2011.

Clinton, Megan. *Smart Girls, Smart Choices: Avoiding the 10 Biggest Mistakes Young Women Make.* Eugene, OR: Harvest House Publishers, 2010.

Copeland, M. Shawn. *Enfleshing Freedom: Body, Race, and Being.* Minneapolis: Fortress Press, 2010.

Crawford, Matthew B. *Shop Class as Soulcraft: An Inquiry into the Value of Work.* New York: Penguin Press, 2009.

———. *The World beyond Your Head: On Becoming an Individual in an Age of Distraction.* New York: Farrar, Straus & Giroux, 2015.

Cuddeback-Gedeon, Lorraine. "Disability: Raising Challenges to Rationality and Embodiment in Theological Anthropology." In *T&T Clark Handbook of Theological Anthropology*, edited by Mary Ann Hinsdale and Stephen Okey, 333–343. New York: Bloomsbury, 2021.

Davis, Patricia H. *Counseling Adolescent Girls.* Minneapolis: Fortress Press, 1996.

Dean, Kenda Creasy. *Almost Christian: What the Faith of Our Teenagers Is Telling the American Church.* Oxford: Oxford University Press, 2010.

DeMoss, Nancy Leigh, and Dannah Gresh. *Lies Young Women Believe and the Truth That Sets Them Free.* Chicago: Moody Publishers, 2008.

DiMarco, Hayley. *Obsessed: Breaking Free from the Things That Consume You.* Grand Rapids, MI: Revell, 2012.

Dittmar, Helga. "The Costs of Consumer Culture and the 'Cage Within': The Impact of the Material 'Good Life' and 'Body Perfect' Ideals on Individuals' Identity and Well-Being." *Psychological Inquiry* 18, no. 1 (March 2007): 23–31.

Dittmar, Helga, Rod Bond, Megan Hurst, and Tim Kasser. "The Relationship between Materialism and Personal Well-Being: A Meta-Analysis." *Journal of Personality and Social Psychology* 107, no. 5 (November 2014): 879–924.

Doak, Mary. "Sex, Race, and Culture: Constructing Theological Anthropology for the Twenty-First Century." *Theological Studies* 80, no. 3 (2019): 508–529.

Downs, Annie F. *Perfectly Unique: Praising God from Head to Toe.* Grand Rapids, MI: Zondervan, 2012.

Driskill, Quo-Li. "Stolen from Our Bodies: First Nations Two-Spirits/ Queers and the Journey to a Sovereign Erotic." In *Feminist and Queer Theology: An Intersectional and Transnational Reader*, edited by L. Ayu Saraswati and Barbara L. Shaw, 443–450. New York: Oxford University Press, 2021.

Dugan, Kate, and Jennifer Owens. "Introduction." In *From the Pews in the Back: Young Women and Catholicism*, edited by Kate Dugan and Jennifer Owens, xv–xxiv. Collegeville, MN: Liturgical Press, 2009.

Eisner, Elliott. *The Educational Imagination: On the Design and Evaluation of School Programs.* 3rd ed. New York: Pearson, 2001.

Elkind, David. *All Grown Up and No Place to Go: Teenagers in Crisis.* Rev. ed. Cambridge, MA: Perseus Books, 1998.

Elliot, Elisabeth. *Passion and Purity: Learning to Bring Your Love Life under Christ's Control.* Grand Rapids, MI: Revell, 2002.

Finke, Leigh. *Queerfully and Wonderfully Made: A Guide for LGBTQ+ Christian Teens.* Minneapolis: Beaming Books, 2020.

Flynn, Andrea. *The Hidden Rules of Race: Barriers to an Inclusive Economy.* New York: Cambridge University Press, 2017.

Fowler, James W. *Stages of Faith: The Psychology of Human Development and the Quest for Meaning.* New ed. San Francisco: HarperOne, 1995.

Freire, Paulo. *Pedagogy of the Oppressed.* Translated by Myra Bergman Ramos. New York: Continuum, 1970.

Freitas, Donna. *The End of Sex: How Hookup Culture Is Leaving a Generation Unhappy, Sexually Unfulfilled, and Confused.* New York: Basic Books, 2013.

———. *Sex and the Soul: Juggling Sexuality, Spirituality, Romance, and Religion on America's College Campuses.* New York: Oxford University Press, 2008.

Giddens, Anthony. *Modernity and Self-Identity: Self and Society in the Late Modern Age.* Stanford, CA: Stanford University Press, 1991.

Gilligan, Carol. *In a Different Voice: Psychological Theory and Women's Development.* Cambridge, MA: Harvard University Press, 1982.

Gonzales, Laurence. *Deep Survival: Who Lives, Who Dies, and Why.* New York: W.W. Norton & Company, 2004.

Gonzalez, Michelle. *Created in God's Image: An Introduction to Feminist Theological Anthropology.* Maryknoll, NY: Orbis Books, 2007.

Griggs, Donald. *Teaching Today's Teachers to Teach.* Nashville: Abingdon Press, 2003.

Groome, Thomas H. *Sharing Faith: A Comprehensive Approach to Religious Education.* San Francisco: HarperSanFrancisco, 1991.

Hamer, Fannie Lou. "'Nobody's Free until Everybody's Free': Speech Delivered at the Founding of the National Women's Political Caucus, Washington, DC, July 10, 1971." In *The Speeches of Fannie Lou Hamer: To Tell It Like It Is,* edited by Maegan Parker Brooks and Davis W. Houck, 134–139. Jackson: University Press of Mississippi, 2011.

Harding, James E. *The Love of David and Jonathan: Ideology, Text, Reception.* New York: Routledge, 2013.

Hinshaw, Stephen, with Rachel Kranz. *The Triple Bind: Saving Our Teenage Girls from Today's Pressures and Conflicting Expectations.* New York: Ballantine Books, 2009.

hooks, bell. *Teaching to Transgress: Education as the Practice of Freedom.* New York: Routledge, 1994.

Isasi-Diaz, Ada Maria. "Kin-Dom of God: A Mujerista Proposal." In *In Our Own Voices: Latino/a Renditions of Theology*, edited by Benjamin Valentin, 171–189. Maryknoll, NY: Orbis Books, 2010.

———. *Mujerista Theology: A Theology for the Twenty-First Century.* Maryknoll, NY: Orbis Books, 1996.

Jennings, Willie James. "Being Baptized: Race." In *The Blackwell Companion to Christian Ethics*, 2nd ed., edited by Stanley Hauerwas and Samuel Wells, 277–289. Oxford: Wiley Blackwell, 2011.

Johnson, Elizabeth A. *She Who Is: The Mystery of God in Feminist Theological Discourse.* 10th anniversary ed. New York: Herder & Herder, 2002.

Josephson-Storm, Jason Ānanda. *Metamodernism: The Future of Theory.* Chicago: The University of Chicago Press, 2021.

Kahm, Emily. "Catholic Girls All Grown Up: A Practical Theological Exploration of Sexuality Formation in Young Adult Women." PhD dissertation, Iliff School of Theology and the University of Denver, 2017.

Kasser, Tim. *The High Price of Materialism.* Cambridge, MA: MIT Press, 2002.

———. "Materialism and Its Alternatives." In *A Life Worth Living: Contributions to Positive Psychology*, edited by Mihaly Csikszentmihalyi and Isabella Celega Csikszentmihalyi, 200–214. Oxford: Oxford University Press, 2006.

Kasser, Tim, Steve Cohn, Allen D. Kanner, and Richard M. Ryan. "Some Costs of American Corporate Capitalism: A Psychological Exploration of Value and Goal Conflicts." *Psychological Inquiry* 18, no. 1 (2007): 1–22. https://doi.org/10.1080/10478400701386579.

Kavanaugh, John F. *Following Christ in a Consumer Society: The Spirituality of Cultural Resistance.* 25th anniversary ed. Maryknoll, NY: Orbis Books, 2006.

Kegan, Robert. *In Over Our Heads: The Mental Demands of Modern Life.* Cambridge, MA: Harvard University Press, 1994.

Kilner, John F. *Dignity and Destiny: Humanity in the Image of God.* Grand Rapids, MI: Eerdmans Publishing, 2015.

Kim, Grace Ji-Sun, and Susan M. Shaw. *Intersectional Theology: An Introductory Guide*. Minneapolis: Fortress Press, 2018.

Kim-Kort, Mihee. *Outside the Lines: How Embracing Queerness Will Transform Your Faith*. Minneapolis: Fortress Press, 2018.

Kinloch, Valerie, and Timothy San Pedro. "The Space between Listening and Storying: Foundations for Projects in Humanization." In *Humanizing Research: Decolonizing Qualitative Inquiry with Youth and Communities*, edited by Django Paris and Maisha T. Winn, 21–42. Thousand Oaks, CA: Sage, 2014.

Klein, Naomi. *No Logo*. 10th anniversary ed. New York: Picador, 2009.

LaCugna, Catherine Mowry. *God for Us: The Trinity and Christian Life*. San Francisco: HarperSanFrancisco, 1992.

Lerner, Richard M. *The Good Teen: Rescuing Adolescence from the Myths of the Storm and Stress Years*. New York: Three Rivers Press, 2007.

Linn, Susan. *Consuming Kids: The Hostile Takeover of Childhood*. New York: New Press, 2004.

Liu, Richard T. "Temporal Trends in the Prevalence of Nonsuicidal Self-Injury among Sexual Minority and Heterosexual Youth from 2005 through 2017." *JAMA Pediatrics* 173, no. 8 (2019): 790–791.

Lookadoo, Justin, and Hayley DiMarco. *Dateable: Are You? Are They?* Grand Rapids, MI: Revell, 2003.

McKnight, John, and Peter Block. *The Abundant Community: Awakening the Power of Families and Neighborhoods*. Chicago: American Planning Association and Berrett-Koehler Publishers, 2010.

Mercer, Joyce Ann. "Calling amid Conflict: What Happens to the Vocations of Youth When Congregations Fight?" In *Greenhouses of Hope: Congregations Growing Young Leaders Who Will Change the World*, edited by Dori Grinenko Baker, 165–190. Herndon, VA: Alban Institute, 2010.

Metz, Johannes Baptist. *Poverty of Spirit*. Rev. ed. New York: Paulist Press, 1998.

Miller, Vincent Jude. *Consuming Religion: Christian Faith and Practice in a Consumer Culture*. New York: Continuum, 2004.

Moder, Gregg. "Bridging Youth Ministry Gaps through Youth Organizing: Actuating Urban Teens as Transformative Community Leaders." *Journal of Youth Ministry* 18, no. 1 (2020): 11–24.

O'Keefe, Theresa A. "Growing Up Alone: The New Normal of Isolation in Adolescence." *The Journal of Youth Ministry* 13, no. 1 (Fall 2014): 63–84.

———. *Navigating toward Adulthood: A Theology of Ministry with Adolescents.* New York: Paulist Press, 2018.

Orenstein, Peggy. *Cinderella Ate My Daughter: Dispatches from the Front Lines of the New Girlie-Girl Culture.* New York: Harper Collins, 2011.

Ott, Kate, and Lorien Carter. "Revisioning Sexuality: Relational Joy and Embodied Flourishing." *Journal of Youth and Theology* 20, no. 1 (2021): 46–64.

Palmer, Parker J. *The Courage to Teach: Exploring the Inner Landscape of a Teacher's Life.* 20th anniversary ed. San Francisco: John Wiley & Sons, 2017.

Putnam, Robert D. *Bowling Alone: The Collapse and Revival of American Community.* Rev. and updated ed. New York: Simon & Schuster, 2020.

———. *Our Kids: The American Dream in Crisis.* New York: Simon & Schuster, 2015.

Pipher, Mary. *Reviving Ophelia: Saving the Selves of Adolescent Girls.* New York: Grosset/Putnam, 1994.

Risch, Gail S., and Michael G. Lawler. "Sexuality Education and the Catholic Teenager: A Report." *Journal of Catholic Education* 7, no. 1 (September 2003): 53–74.

Roche, Mary M. Doyle. *Children, Consumerism, and the Common Good.* Lanham, MD: Lexington Books, 2009.

Root, Andrew. *Faith Formation in a Secular Age: Responding to the Church's Obsession with Youthfulness.* Ada, MI: Baker Academic, 2017.

Saiving, Valerie. "The Human Situation: A Feminine View." In *Womanspirit Rising: A Feminist Reader in Religion*, edited by Carol P. Christ and Judith Plaskow, 25–42. San Francisco: Harper & Row, 1979.

Sales, Nancy Jo. *American Girls: Social Media and the Secret Lives of Teenagers.* New York: Alfred Knopf, 2016.

Sanders, Cody J. *A Brief Guide to Ministry with LGBTQIA Youth.* Louisville, KY: Westminster John Knox Press, 2017.

Santelli, John S., Stephanie A. Grilo, Laura D. Lindberg, Ilene S. Speizer, Amy Schalet, Jennifer Heitel, Leslie M. Kantor et al. "Abstinence-Only-Until-Marriage Policies and Programs: An Updated Position Paper of the Society for Adolescent Health and Medicine." *Journal of Adolescent Health* 61, no. 3 (September 2017): 400–403.

Saracino, Michele. *Christian Anthropology: An Introduction to the Human Person.* New York: Paulist Press, 2015.

Schor, Juliet. *Born to Buy: The Commercialized Child and the New Consumer Culture.* New York: Scribner, 2004.

———. *The Overworked American: The Unexpected Decline of Leisure.* New York: Basic Books, 1991.

———. *Plenitude: The New Economics of True Wealth.* New York: Penguin Press, 2010.

Shepherd, Sheri Rose. *His Princess: Girl Talk with God.* Grand Rapids, MI: Fleming H. Revell, 2010.

Shrum, L. J., Nancy Wong, Farrah Arif, Sunaina K. Chugani, Alexander Gunz, Tina M. Lowrey, Agnes Nairn et al. "Reconceptualizing Materialism as Identity Goal Pursuits: Functions, Processes, and Consequences." In "Recent Advances in Globalization, Culture and Marketing Strategy," edited by Michel Laroche and Seong-Yeon Park. Special issue, *Journal of Business Research* 66, no. 8 (August 2013): 1179–1185.

Simmons, Rachel. *The Curse of the Good Girl: Raising Authentic Girls with Courage and Confidence.* New York: Penguin Press, 2009.

Sledge, Robert W. "The Saddest Day: Gene Leggett and the Origins of the Incompatible Clause." *Methodist History* 55, no. 3 (2017): 145–179.

Soelle, Dorothee. *Suffering.* Philadelphia: Fortress Press, 1984.

Straus, Martha B. *Adolescent Girls in Crisis: Intervention and Hope.* New York: W.W. Norton, 2007.

Taylor, Charles. *The Ethics of Authenticity*. Cambridge, MA: Harvard University Press, 1992.

———. *A Secular Age*. Cambridge, MA: Harvard University Press, 2007.

Thistle, Susan. *From Marriage to the Market: The Transformation of Women's Lives and Work*. Berkeley: University of California Press, 2006.

Turkle, Sherry. *Alone Together: Why We Expect More from Technology and Less from Each Other*. New York: Basic Books, 2011.

Twenge, Jean M., and Eric Farley. "Not All Screen Time Is Created Equal: Associations with Mental Health Vary by Activity and Gender." *Social Psychiatry and Psychiatric Epidemiology* 56, no. 2 (February 1, 2021): 207–217.

Twenge, Jean M., and Tim Kasser. "Generational Changes in Materialism and Work Centrality, 1976–2007: Associations with Temporal Changes in Societal Insecurity and Materialistic Role Modeling." *Personality & Social Psychology Bulletin* 39, no. 7 (2013): 883–897.

Warren, Michael. *Youth, Gospel, Liberation*. San Francisco: Harper & Row, 1987.

Weaver, Darlene Fozard. "Sin and the Subversion of Ethics: Why the Discourse of Sin Is Good for Theological Anthropology." In *The T&T Clark Handbook of Theological Anthropology*, edited by Mary Ann Hinsdale and Stephen Okey, 99–110. New York: Bloomsbury, 2021.

White, David F. *Practicing Discernment with Youth: A Transformative Youth Ministry Approach*. Cleveland, OH: Pilgrim Press, 2005.

Williams, Neil H. *The Maleness of Jesus: Is It Good News for Women?* Eugene, OR: Cascade Books, 2011.

Wimberly, Anne Streaty. *Soul Stories: African American Christian Education*. Nashville: Abingdon Press, 1994.

Woznicki, Andrew N. *A Christian Humanism: Karol Wojtyla's Existential Personalism*. New Britain, CT: Mariel Publications, 1980.

Zuboff, Shoshana. *The Age of Surveillance Capitalism: The Fight for a Human Future at the New Frontier of Power*. New York: PublicAffairs, 2019.